HEROES OF
THE RAF

Douglas Bader

by Michael Evans

First Published 2014
Text Copyright © Michael Evans 2014
All rights reserved. No reproduction of any part of this
publication is permitted without the prior written
permission of the publisher:
Bretwalda Books
Unit 8, Fir Tree Close, Epsom,
Surrey KT17 3LD
info@BretwaldaBooks.com
www.BretwaldaBooks.com
To receive an e-catalogue of our complete
range of books send an email to
info@BretwaldaBooks.com
ISBN 978-1-909698-12-3

Printed and bound in Great Britain by
Marston Book Services Limited, Oxfordshire

Mention the name of Douglas Bader and most people will know who you are talking about even though a considerable number were not even born when he died on 5th September 1982. Yet in many respects he is just as famous now as he was when he was alive.

So what was it about this man that makes him so unforgettable?

When he was 21 he was a talented sportsman who had played cricket at the Oval and rugby at Twickenham. He was tipped for an England cap at rugby and he was one of the top aerobatic display pilots of the RAF. Then tragedy struck. While he was giving an impromptu aerobatic display he had an accident where he lost both of his legs.

As a result of a mixture of determination, courage and often sheer bloody-mindedness, he overcame what to many others would have been a crippling disability and went on to become a charismatic and inspirational leader, a fighter pilot of distinction and a thorn in the side of his captors after he became a POW.

In the post-war period, during his 23 years working with Shell, he travelled the world in his single-engine aircraft, clocking up an impressive 3,900 flying hours and when he retired it was said that no other pilot in the world had greater all-round experience of flying and navigating light aircraft.

On his many trips he always took the opportunity to devote time to people with disabilities. To a great many he was an inspiration and a wonderful example of a way that a disability could be overcome.

After his death a number of his family and friends formed the Douglas Bader Foundation to continue Douglas's work in the advancement and promotion of the physical, mental and spiritual welfare of persons who had lost limbs or who were otherwise disabled.

One of the features of the Foundation is its annual golf tournament. Douglas had been a very good golfer and very early on he had discovered that as long as he remained fit and there was strength in his body, his legs, or lack of them, would never stop him from doing what he set his mind to do.

The Formative Years

To say that Douglas Bader was a complex character would be a grave understatement. He was undoubtedly different things to different people and some people saw him as self-opinionated, self-centred, outspoken, dogmatic, reckless, exasperating and a person who was capable of generating extreme dislike.

He was certainly all of these, but he was also a charismatic and inspirational leader, defiant in the face of adversity and extremely brave and tenacious in the pursuit of his enemies. He could also be charming, inspirational, generous with his time and compassionate. His many friendships were loyal and lasting and he was someone who could be excellent company. His extreme self-confidence enabled him to inspire confidence and admiration in others.

To understand Douglas Robert Steuart Bader it is necessary to look at his childhood. He was born on 21st February 1910 in St John's Wood in London, the second son of Frederick and Jessie Bader. His father was a civil engineer and shortly after Douglas's birth his father returned to work in India taking his wife and Douglas's elder brother with him. The

A Bristol Bulldog biplane fighter. The aircraft entered service in 1929 and was retired in 1937. For its day it was an effective fighter with twin machine guns and a top speed of 178mph.

young Douglas had been suffering from measles and was not considered fit enough for the journey so he was sent to live with relatives on the Isle of Man where he spent the next two years.

When Douglas was two it was decided that he should join his parents in India, but the following year his father resigned his job and in 1913 the family returned to England and settled in Kew.   It was not a happy household. Robert Bader was 20 years older than his wife and they were constantly fighting. There was also fierce rivalry between Douglas and his older brother Derick.

During the Great War Douglas's father was commissioned in the Royal Engineers, but was wounded in the head during an action in 1917. By the end of the war he had reached the rank of major and stayed in France working for the War Graves Commission. Douglas and his family saw little of him during this time

Just after his eleventh birthday Douglas went to stay with his mother's sister Hazel and her husband Cyril Burge. Douglas's Uncle Cyril was adjutant at the Royal Air Force College at Cranwell. The sport-mad eleven-year-old boy had a wonderful time and the whole place had a lasting effect on him.

While at his prep school in Eastbourne, Douglas had discovered sport as a way of making best use of his pent-up energy and by the age of 12 he was captain of rugby, football and cricket. He was also an excellent athlete, winning every race that he ran.

In 1922 Frederick Bader died from complications of the wounds that he had received five years earlier. This was potentially a financial disaster for the family and soon after her husband's death Jessie Bader, who was still only 32, remarried.

Her new husband was the Revd Ernest William Hobbs, the Rector of the parish of St Mary the Virgin, Spotborough, near Doncaster in the West Riding of Yorkshire. Mr Hobbs was a mild-mannered man and was far from being the strong father figure that Douglas or his brother required.

The two brothers bitterly resented having to move to Yorkshire and became largely out of control and during that first summer holiday Douglas was packed off to stay with relatives.

It was towards the end of the holiday when Douglas and Derick were both back at the rectory in Spotborough that a bitter argument broke out between them that resulted in Derick shooting Douglas at close range with an air gun and hitting him in the shoulder.

Having been made aware that after the death of his father family funds were short, Douglas studied hard and won a scholarship to St Edward's School in Oxford. Once he started at St Edward's Douglas's competitive sprit seemed to take control. He showed little interest in academic subjects, but at sports he excelled. By the age of fifteen he was the youngest member of the school rugby team and in his final year he was captain of the first fifteen. In the spring of 1928 he was also captain of cricket.

The urge to compete always seemed to be uppermost, as was the desire to lead. Whenever there was an element of contest he would throw himself in. He enjoyed debating as well as sports and somehow managed to dominate everything that he took part in.

He was also fiercely loyal to all those who showed that they had faith in him, like his sports master who applauded the boy's breezy commitment and infectious enthusiasm and the effects that these had on the other members of the teams. Then there was his headmaster who in spite of some disapproval, had been astute enough to take a tolerant view of Douglas's sometimes-unpredictable behaviour and had made him a prefect.

The years had passed and the time was fast approaching when Douglas had to consider his future and it was a visit to the school by an old boy who was a cadet at the RAF College at Cranwell that set him thinking about the RAF as a career.

Douglas remembered the very enjoyable holiday at Cranwell with his uncle and aunt and he wrote to his uncle about the possibility of becoming an air force officer.

The main College Hall at RAF Cranwell. It was at Cranwell that Bader was trained to be an RAF officer, a function that Cranwell still performs in the 21st century.

There were two major problems. The first was that the family would not be able to afford the fees and the second was that Douglas's mother was very much opposed to the idea of him joining the RAF, but his Uncle Cyril supported him and knew of a way that would be very likely to give Douglas what he wanted.

Cyril Burge was now personal assistant to the Chief of Air Staff and he knew the sort of answers that the selection board wanted to hear. He sent his nephew a set of questions and model answers. Since there would be a problem of affording fees, he also told Douglas that each year the College offered six prize scholarships through competitive examination and he suggested that Douglas might try for one of these. Douglas's competitive sprit was fired up and after scoring a total of 235 points out of 250 at the selection board, he crammed like fury and managed to win the fifth of the six scholarships.

Douglas loved his two years at Cranwell. He learnt to fly and found that he loved being a pilot. There was plenty of sport and while he continued to excel at rugby and cricket, he also discovered an aptitude for hockey and boxing. Sadly his interest in his academic subjects did not match his other interests and at the end of his first year he came very close to being expelled.

Things had begun to mount up. Douglas had already gained quite a reputation among the staff for his wild antics and then he was caught yet again joy riding in a banned personal car. As if that was not enough, he had come nineteenth out of twenty-one in the written exams for his class.

Fortunately the commandant, Air Vice-Marshall Halahan, appreciated Douglas's potential leadership qualities and gave him a last chance after quietly warning him that the RAF wanted adults for its officers, not overgrown adolescents.

"Bader," he reportedly said, "I just want you to understand that we're getting a bit sick of you and your friends. This isn't a sort of school. What we want in the Royal Air Force are men, not boys." There was a long pause. "That's all."

His two years passed very quickly. Cranwell in those days was very much a bachelor existence. There was a convention that no man married until he either became a Squadron Leader or reached the age of 30, which effectively ruled out married cadets. This led to a degree of wild behaviour. One of his great friends was fellow cadet Geoffrey Stephenson. Their paths were to cross a number of times during the future course of their careers.

Cadets were not permitted to own cars, but they were allowed motorbikes and brushes with the law were fairly regular. Fortunately the local police were very understanding and little was ever heard about incidents that involved Cranwell cadets.

Douglas's final report at Cranwell summed him up as "plucky, capable and headstrong" and he was commissioned as a Pilot Officer on 26th July 1930 having just missed being awarded the Sword of Honour for best cadet. He came second to Patrick Coote, who Douglas described as "a splendid man; very good all round - at games, at work, at flying, at everything."

On 13th April 1941 Patrick Coote, by then a Wing Commander, was killed in Greece while flying as an observer in a 211 Squadron Bristol Blenheim during a low-level attack against the enemy.

Douglas and Geoffrey Stephenson were both posted to 23 Squadron at RAF Kenley. This was in a delightful spot situated roughly between Croydon and Caterham. The squadron was equipped with the Gloster Gamecock, a nippy little single-seat biplane that although rather unstable, was just right for aerobatics.

Douglas bought himself an MG sports car and he later described his time at Kenley as "the most enormous fun". He was selected for the RAF cricket team, playing at the Oval and other top grounds against the other two services, university teams and the MCC. He played rugby for the RAF, Combined Services and Harlequins at Twickenham and was firmly tipped for an England cap.

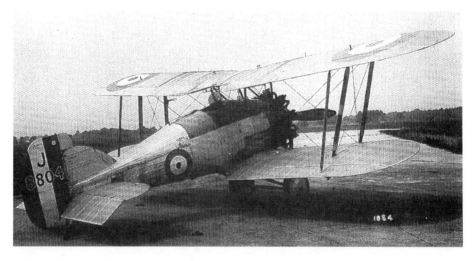

The Gloster Gamecock fighter. This nimble aircraft had its twin machine guns mounted internally and could reach 155mph, but it suffered reliability problems and so was withdrawn from service sooner than intended.

Douglas continued to be fiercely competitive and although he loved his sport, there was an element of frustration because it kept him away from flying. He was very keen to be chosen for the select band of pilots who took part in the aerobatic displays at the annual Hendon Air Pageant.

In 1931 23 Squadron's Gloster Gamecocks were being replaced with the faster but less agile Bristol Bulldog. The Gamecocks were much better at performing aerobatics and it was decided that they would perform one last time. It was Douglas's good fortune that his flight was the last one in the RAF to operate the Gamecock and so he was chosen to take part in the display with Flight Lieutenant Harry Day. Geoffrey Stephenson was first reserve.

It was a thrilling 15-minute aerobatic display that left the crowd of 170,000 completely spellbound. Two months later Douglas and Geoffrey Stephenson appeared together for the first time and soon established a reputation for themselves for aerobatic skills that were beyond the reach of all but a small handful of service pilots.

Without a doubt Douglas was a daredevil when it came to aerobatics, especially at low levels. Although they were not supposed to do aerobatics in the Gamecock below 500 feet, Douglas's flight commander often turned a blind eye when he saw him doing slow rolls at near-ground level.

The low-level rule became more important after the remainder of 23 Squadron converted to Bristol Bulldogs. These were fine aircraft in their time, but they had problems with directional stability at low speeds. This made low-level aerobatics particularly dangerous and strict instructions were issued forbidding this.

To Douglas this was yet another petty restriction, but in truth the survival rate among the former Hendon pairs was very poor. In the second half of the year there had been 27 accidents, seven of them fatal, all because the standing orders had been ignored.

The Royal Berkshire Hospital. Bader was treated here after his accident. The hospital had been founded in 1839 by Viscount Sidmouth and by the time Bader arrived in 1931 was one of the top hospitals outside London.

Douglas was convinced that his view was correct and he was supported by Harry Day, who by then was temporary CO of 23 Squadron. Day's view was that regulations were only necessary for those too stupid to understand their own limits, but he did go so far as to warn Douglas about "showing off".

It was on Monday 14th December 1931 that disaster struck. One of the 23 Squadron pilots, Flying Officer Geoffrey Phillips, had a brother who was involved in the aero club at the civilian airfield at Woodley, near Reading. He had been invited to lunch with his brother and suggested that Douglas and Geoffrey Stephenson accompanied him.

They had had their Bristol Bulldogs for two or three months and they were really getting used to them. Douglas, for instance had completed 32 hours and 20 minutes on Bulldogs and this flight would add to his total.

The three pilots flew to Woodley and had lunch. Various stories exist as to what followed next. One thing that is without doubt is that the three pilots decided to give their hosts a little display. During this, Douglas flew very low and the wingtip of his Bulldog hit the ground, causing it to cartwheel into the earth. It was an error of only two or three feet, but it was catastrophic.

Apart from a badly gashed face and two broken ribs, both his legs were badly smashed up. He was bleeding profusely from a severed femoral artery, but fortunately Jack Cruttenden, one of the civilian pupil pilots, had learnt enough first aid at home in Australia to know how to stop Douglas from bleeding to death.

Douglas was rushed to the Royal Berkshire Hospital in Reading with Jack Cruttenden pressing his thumbs down on the femoral artery of Douglas's right knee to stop the flow of blood. It was his good fortune to arrive at the hospital just before the prominent surgeon J Leonard Joyce left for the day. Joyce was one of the best orthopaedic surgeons in the country and he immediately decided that in order to save Douglas's life the right leg must be amputated at once above the knee.

Two days later Douglas's other leg also had to be removed, but this time it was possible to save the knee.

There were three things that helped to save Douglas's life; one was his supreme physical fitness, another was his courage and a third was his sheer determination. The more he heard that nothing could be done for him, the more resolute he became to prove to these doubters that nothing could stand between him and his chosen goals.

Something that sharpened his resolve was when he was passing in and out of consciousness a few days after his accident and he heard a nurse asking for quiet in the corridor outside his room because, "there's a boy dying in there." His immediate reaction in his semi-comatose state was "No there's not!"

On Christmas Eve 1931 he was moved to a nursing home called Gracelands where he was put under the care of a nurse called Dorothy Brace. Douglas always called her 'Brace' and she was a tower of strength to him. When he was fitted with his first peg leg and kept falling over, she just said: "Take it easy - and I do wish you wouldn't use that appalling language."

After four months in hospital in Reading, he transferred to the RAF hospital in Uxbridge and was soon able to travel to Roehampton to be fitted with a set of aluminium artificial legs. He initially found these incredibly difficult to use and when he was told that he would never be able to walk without a stick, his reply was: "I'll never never walk with a stick" and he never did.

Six months after his accident he was astounding the staff at Roehampton by stumping about unaided, if a trifle erratically, on artificial legs. His determination was obviously the key, but his sporty background was a tremendous asset. He had a games player's balance and thanks to his early gymnastic training he had no fear of falling over.

When he did fall, and this often happened in the early stages, he always tended to fall forwards and his powerful hands, arms and shoulders helped him to save himself. He refused to allow any trace of self-pity and was able to turn pathos into laughter and even hilarity and use this to play off any embarrassment.

He could be very obstinate and was not averse to telling anyone who was being the faintest bit defeatist that they didn't know what the hell they were talking about. This upset some people who were simply trying to help him and thought that he was being rude and inconsiderate.

Douglas on the other hand was of the opinion that he had been given this new equipment and it was up to him to get on with it. He was on his own and it was up to him to live with his problems and make his own way.

Towards the summer of 1932, about nine months after his accident and having had the pedals of his car altered, Douglas was already driving again and he was beginning to think of flying. Sir Philip Sassoon, Under Secretary of State for Air took a personal interest in him and arranged for him to fly an Avro 504 with one of the members of 601 County of London Auxiliary Air Force Squadron.

Flying proved to be no problem, but the question was how would the RAF react. Sassoon helped things along. A medical board passed him fit for dual flying only and he was sent to the RAF Central Flying School for four weeks to see if he could fly aeroplanes to the necessary standard. The chief flying instructor told him that he was wasting his time there and that he could fly perfectly well and that he intended to say so.

Unfortunately this cut no ice as far as the medical board's decision was concerned. An officer without legs could not fly solo - the rules effectively said as much. If that was the case, fumed Douglas, why did they send him to the Central Flying School in the first place? Presumably they thought that he would fail and that this would let them off the hook.

In the event Douglas was posted to RAF Duxford where to his horror he was put in charge of motor transport. Not only had his accident deprived him of his beloved sport and banned him from flying solo, but all the RAF seemed able to offer him was this dead end job.

This was a very unsettling time for Douglas and in the summer of 1933 he and the RAF decided to part company. He received a small disability pension, but he needed a job. With no training, other than that as an RAF officer, he was fortunate to get a position with the Asiatic Petroleum Company, which later became part of Shell. His annual salary was £200, which was most useful, because on 15th October that year he was secretly married to Thelma Edwards in Hampstead Registry Office.

They had first met while Douglas was still a patient at Uxbridge. He and two friends had decided to go for an afternoon drive. They were a bizarre-looking trio; one with his broken arm in plaster, one with a broken leg in plaster and Douglas of course with no legs at all. They stopped at a roadside restaurant where, more or less for something to do, Thelma was working as a part-time waitress.

Douglas and Thelma immediately hit it off and they began to see more of each other. When he visited her family for the first time she stressed to her young brother and sister that on no account should they mention Douglas's legs. They dutifully kept silent, but it was clear that they were both fascinated by them and couldn't tear their eyes away. Douglas said nothing, but solemnly took out his pipe and tapped it out on his knee. There was a loud metallic ring. Douglas let out a great guffaw of laughter, the ice was broken and things never looked back.

After they were married Thelma became very much a human rock on which Douglas could lean. This became very important during his time working at Shell. He found the office work humdrum in the extreme, but one consolation was that during this time he discovered golf.

Once he had mastered the technique of teeing off without falling over, he proved beyond doubt that he could make himself into a good enough golfer to be able to play anywhere and with anyone. He had discovered that as long as he remained fit and there was strength in his body, his legs, or lack of them, would never stop him from doing what he set his mind to.

The Onset of Total War

The 1930s was a golden period for flying. It was the time of great pioneers of long-distance solo flight, such as Amy Johnson, Jim Mollison, Jean Batten, Kingsford Smith and Campbell Black. Commercial air transport was in its infancy but Imperial Airways, Lufthansa and KLM were already making their presence felt.

Parallel to all this was the increase in the military might of Germany and as international tensions mounted, Douglas began to badger just about everyone he knew who could have the slightest influence in getting him reinstated in the RAF and back to flying again.

A great ally was his old friend Geoffrey Stephenson, who by now was a staff officer at Adastral House, home of the Air Ministry in London's Kingsway. Stephenson beavered away for Douglas behind the scenes and was a great help.

Thelma was dead against all this. She was horrified at the possibility of Douglas being shot down and trapped in a crashing aircraft because of his legs. Thelma's mother agreed with her. To her, what her dogmatic and aggressive son-in-law was proposing to do was both unnecessary and unreasonable. All that it was doing was causing Thelma endless turmoil and distress.

Douglas was resolute. He had always believed that if you wanted something badly enough, the way to get it was to go right to the top so he wrote to the Air Member for Personnel, Air Marshal Charles Portal.

On 31st August, days before the outbreak of war, Portal wrote a personal reply to Douglas. Although he told Douglas he was too busy to see him and that he was not able to employ him at the present time, in the event of war a new situation would arise and Douglas would almost certainly be used in a flying capacity, provided the doctors agreed.

Although positive, in a guarded sort of way, this was still not enough for Douglas. What he was looking for was immediate acceptance and his next target was Air Vice-Marshall Fredrick Halahan, his old commandant from Cranwell. Halahan obviously remembered Douglas and wrote to the head of the medical board at the Air Ministry saying that in his opinion Bader was the sort of officer the service needed and if found fit, apart from his legs, he should immediately be sent to the Central Flying School and given a chance to prove himself.

So off Douglas headed for the Central Flying School at Uphaven where, by good fortune, the instructor who was given the task of assessing Douglas was another old friend from Cranwell, Rupert Leigh, now a Squadron Leader. Needless to say, Douglas passed with flying colours.

By now Britain was at war and with pilots being urgently needed, earlier concerns had been overridden. It was accepted that Douglas should rejoin as a fully operational pilot, although it was stressed that in view of possible problems with his legs he should not form part of an aircrew, but should be posted to a Spitfire or Hurricane squadron. This, of course, was exactly what Douglas wanted.

In November 1939 he learnt that he was to be reinstated as a Flying Officer and once again was sent back to the Central Flying School for a refresher course. By the third week in December he had graduated to flying a single-seat Hawker Hurricane in which, according to his logbook, he promptly did aerobatics. He also took the opportunity of flying over to Duxford, where Geoffrey Stephenson was now CO of No. 19 Squadron with its Spitfire Mk Is.

It was perhaps no coincidence that he chose the day that Air Vice-Marshall Trafford Leigh-Mallory, AOC of 12 (Fighter) Group was visiting Duxford. The officer in charge of flying operations, Squadron Leader A B 'Woody' Woodhall, had known Douglas during his time with 23 Squadron at Kenley and he introduced Douglas to the AOC.

An RAF Spitfire has its guns callibrated in between flights. The RAF at first adopted a scattergun approach, but early combats soon showed the value of having the guns set up so that they formed a deadly cone of converging fire.

According to Woody, Douglas and the AOC were mutually attracted to each other and what was later to become a firm friendship between the two men was established at that first meeting. They were, said Woody, "two of a kind - born leaders and respected by all and affectionately esteemed by most". After lunch Douglas treated everyone to a display of aerobatics and this confirmed to the AOC that here was someone who was worth fostering.

On 7th February 1940 Douglas received his posting to 19 Squadron and returned to Duxford. As he was later to say, "I left the Royal Air Force at Duxford and I came back into it at Duxford, through the same bloody gate."

Douglas as ever was full of self-confidence and in his own mind he was a far better pilot than many of the other members of 19 Squadron. Many regarded him with a mixture of awe and inspiration, but others who had to fly with him were not always so impressed. In spite of his great natural

A Hawker Hurricane MkI photographed before the war. With a top speed of 324mph and armed with 8 machine guns the rugged Hurricane was a far more modern and effective fighter than anything Bader had flown before.

talent, he took longer to master flying a Spitfire in varying conditions than he was keen to admit. Several times his over-confidence resulted in embarrassing incidents.

When a Pilot Officer was giving him a cockpit briefing for his first Spitfire flight, Douglas, already familiar with flying a Hurricane and anxious to get airborne, had impatiently brushed him aside. He took off before the Pilot Officer had the chance to explain the procedures for lowering the undercarriage and as if this wasn't enough, he had not listened properly while the radio procedures were being explained to him.

After a very exhilarating flight, as he returned to Duxford, Douglas realised that he did not know how to lower the undercarriage. Not only this, but he didn't know how to radio for assistance in order to ask. Fortunately he managed to sort things out by trial and error, but it was a scary experience.

A few days later he practised formation flying for the first time as part of a three-aircraft 'vic' led by Flight Lieutenant Brian Lane. He decided to demonstrate how good he was by tucking himself only three feet or so behind his leader's wing. This required a great deal of concentration and as they were coming in to land, it was only at the last minute that Douglas saw a hut in front of him. He managed to pull up in time, but still lost his tail wheel.

He blamed Brian Lane for this, saying that he had chosen a guide path too close to a building - and he didn't hesitate to tell him so.

On another occasion, a month or so after joining 19 Squadron, Douglas was taking off from Horsham St Faiths, just outside Norwich. The squadron had been taking part in North Sea patrol work and as this was too far from Duxford they would set of for Horsham St Faiths before first light, spend the day there mounting patrols and then return to Duxford late in the evening. It was an exhausting day.

On this occasion Douglas neglected to set his propeller to fine pitch for take off. This would give the aircraft more grip and result in a shorter take off run. As a result of this error, the Spitfire didn't gain enough speed to get airborne. Had he been more experienced he would have noticed his error, but he ended up crashing into the boundary fence.

The aircraft was a complete write-off and Douglas's metal legs were badly damaged, but if they had been real ones he would probably have died. Even so the ignominy of the situation was horrible for Douglas. He had a spare set of legs but they were a bit uncomfortable and while he was filing away at the metal in the middle of the night in an attempt to trim them a bit, the continual scraping noise began to get on the nerves of Flight Sergeant George Unwin.

The new Walt Disney film Snow White and the Seven Dwarfs has just been released and when Unwin complained, Douglas's retort was: "Oh shut up Grumpy!" The name stuck and even when he was later a Group Captain, George Unwin was still known as Grumpy, although not always to his face.

Douglas found the Spitfire quite a joy to fly. It was more than twice as fast as the Bulldog biplanes of 23 Squadron and one evening, when nobody else was about, he slipped off to do a little 20-minute test flight in his aircraft. When he returned to Duxford he couldn't resist repeating the same manoeuvre that had resulted in his crash at Woodley, just below hanger height. He did it perfectly and made a perfect landing.

As Douglas walked back across the tarmac, a figure emerged from the gloom. It was Wing Commander "Pingo" Lester, the station commander. "Oh Douglas," he pleaded, "I do wish that you wouldn't do that. You had such a nasty accident last time."

Douglas was not 100% happy while he was with 19 Squadron. He was quite a bit older than many of the other pilots and not to put too finer point on it, his supreme self-confidence made him feel that he was better qualified than many of the other pilots and anyway, he liked to be 'in charge'.

He was delighted when in April 1940, Squadron Leader 'Tubby' Mermagen, another old friend from his Cranwell days, asked him to take over B Flight of 222 (Natal) Squadron that was also stationed at Duxford.

222 Squadron had been flying two-engined Blenheim Mk IFs, but were about to re-equip with Spitfires. 19 year-old Tim Vigors joined the squadron direct from Cranwell and flying training school at about that time. He remembered Douglas as: " broad-shouldered, dark-haired, determined looking flight lieutenant much older than any of us."

" 'Are you Vigors?" he asked with his piercing blue eyes looking straight into mine.

" 'That's me,' I replied, holding his gaze.

" 'You've been put in my flight. Come on over to my office. I want to talk to you.' "

After some preliminary chitchat about Cranwell and the flying training school, Douglas asked Vigors his first name.

" 'Tim,' I said.

" 'I don't like unnecessary formality and you and I have got a lot of work to do during the next few weeks. So, call me Douglas.' "

Although this informality was typical of Douglas, there was never any doubt about who was boss and woe betide anyone who tried to take advantage. Tim Vigors and Douglas actually became very good friends and during that time Tim began to see a great deal of Thelma's sister Jill.

There was a need for the squadron's new aircraft to be collected from the factory and Douglas knew that Tim had trained on single-engined Gloster Gladiators, while the rest of the squadron had been used to flying twin-engined Blenheims. Apart from Douglas and Tubby Mergmagen he was the only pilot experienced at flying single engined aircraft.

After being given a quick course on flying a Spitfire, Tim then joined Douglas in flying to the factory in Southampton in an Avro Anson, where they each collected a new Spitfire and flew it back to Duxford. Apart from two days when they were grounded by bad weather, this shuttle process lasted for a whole week until nearly all the squadron was fully equipped.

222 Squadron soon got used to their new Spitfires and training was relentless. The other member of Douglas's flight was Tim's room mate Hilary Edridge. In his autobiography Tim wrote how he and Hilary practiced with Douglas until they could fly in tight formation and manoeuvre with their wing tips a mere ten feet from Douglas's aircraft and their propellers dangerously close to his wing tips.

Douglas was very critical of the tactics that Fighter Command had developed. These tactics were based on the assumption that any attack on Britain would be in the form of a bomber force coming from the North Sea. There would be no fighter escort, partly because the North Sea crossing was beyond fighter range, but also because it was considered that the defensive armament of a bomber did not require an escort.

As a result, RAF tactics were effectively a series of highly choreographed attack formations designed to intercept approaching unescorted enemy bomber formations.

A flight of Squadron No.19 Spitfires in their pre-war livery. The Spitfire was 30mph faster than the Hurricane, could climb faster and was more nimble in combat. Bader was only one of many pilots to love the "Spit".

Any combats between fighters were expected to involve RAF aircraft flying from French air fields. At that time it was regarded as being inconceivable that France would ever be overrun by invading forces following the building of the massive fortress line that the French had built along their border with Germany.

Douglas had studied the aerial battle techniques of fighters during the Great War and he was convinced that instead of these carefully choreographed formations the best form of attack was as he put it, for everyone to "pile in together from each side as close to the Hun as they can and let him have the lot".

As ever, Douglas was not slow in voicing his opinions, but as Geoffrey Stephenson pointed out to him in March 1940, there was no way of telling if the Air Ministry had got it wrong. Admittedly there was a chance that Douglas had actually got it right, but as Geoffrey said: "you don't know do you?"

When Geoffrey was shot down on his very first mission, he found out to his cost that there had actually been a lot of truth in the views that Douglas had been putting forward.

Training was interspersed with boring North Sea patrols, but this all came to an end after the Wehrmacht launched its invasion of Luxembourg, Belgium, the Netherlands and France on 10th May.

By then Woody had been promoted Wing Commander and was now Sector Controller at Duxford in addition to being Station Commander. The period after the German invasion of the Low Countries was the start of a busy time for the Duxford squadrons.

264 Squadron initially had great success with their Boulton Paul Defiants. From the front the Defiants bore a strong resemblance to single seater Hurricanes. In fact they were actually two-seater aircraft and although they had no forward-facing armament, they had four machine guns in a rear-facing turret.

When the enemy first attacked them from behind in the usual way, they were blasted out of the sky. On their very first mission the six Defiants shot down twelve enemy aircraft for no loss. The British press was jubilant and pictures of the Defiants were published that showed the rear-facing armament and explaining the reasons for their success.

By the time the Defiants next went into action, the Luftwaffe had realised its earlier mistake and this time the attacks came from the front. Without being able to defend themselves, Defiant casualties were heavy and in due course they were withdrawn from daylight operations entirely. After they had been painted black they became reasonable night fighters.

Meanwhile the French Air Force was suffering heavy losses. Winston Churchill had taken over as British Prime Minister on 10th May and the French Government appealed to him for 10 RAF squadrons to help them out. Churchill was not particularly pleased when Air Chief Marshall Hugh Dowding, C-in-C of Fighter Command initially refused. Dowding was very conscious of the fact that if he committed all of his resources to the defence of France, he could very well find himself in the position of not having anything left for a later defence of Britain.

Air Vice Marshal Hugh Dowding commanded RAF Fighter Command from 1936 to the end of 1940, and so throughout the Battle of Britain. Bader did not see eye to eye with Dowding over tactics to be used in the Battle of Britain.

In the autumn of 1939 the Air Ministry's estimated requirement for home defence was 52 squadrons, but at that time only 34 in all states of efficiency were available. Another great shortage was trained pilots. It took about a year to train a pilot and Dowding knew that he could not afford to squander them away.

In the event, six additional Hurricane squadrons were sent to France the following day, but Dowding insisted that the precious Spitfires should be kept in reserve in Britain. Douglas and the other members of the Duxford Spitfire squadrons had to wait impatiently until nearly the end of the month before they saw any action

On 25th May 19 Squadron flew down to Hornchurch and the following day they met the enemy for the first time. Approximately ten enemy aircraft were shot down, but on that first day 19 Squadron lost two of their number, one being the CO, Geoffrey Stephenson. Geoffrey was a brilliant pilot, but one who flew by the book. The book said that aircraft were to fly in tight formations and the loss of Geoffrey seemed to provide conclusive proof that it was the book rather than Douglas that had been wrong.

As George 'Grumpy' Unwin later commented, "our tight formations were all very well for the Hendon Air Pageant, but useless in combat. Geoffrey Stephenson was a prime example; without modern combat experience he flew by the book - and was in effect shot down by it".

Geoffrey Stephenson became a POW and for a time he was Senior British Officer at Stalag Luft I, located near the small Baltic seaport town of Barth. After making multiple escape attempts from different camps he was eventually transferred to Oflag IV-C, better known as Colditz Castle, where he was actively involved in the design and construction of the Colditz Cock glider. This was to have been used in an escape attempt, but the war ended before it could be put to the test.

Early on 28th May 222 Squadron was finally called to action when it was ordered down to Martlesham Heath near Ipswich. It was here that for the first time Douglas met another of the future great wartime aces, Robert Stanford Tuck. Tuck and the remainder of 92 Squadron had been in action for some time and had already lost more than enough friends killed over the Dunkirk beaches.

The two men did not hit it off. Bader's self-confidence grated on Tuck. "I remember that my immediate reaction to this rather obstreperous man who came up to me that morning was that he was too cocky," Tuck later recalled.

To Douglas's great disappointment 222 Squadron saw no action that morning and were diverted to Hornchurch where it was the turn of pilots of 54 and 65 Squadrons to have the treat of meeting Douglas for the first time. Flight Lieutenant Gordon Olive recalled many years later how Douglas immediately took charge of the conversation. He had gazed with mild derision at the 54 Squadron pilots with their stubbly chins and the pistols that they carried, which he took as Hollywood-style showing off, rather than the results of being forced to watch friends parachuting into enemy-held territory.

New Zealander Al Deere, a member of 54 Squadron, who had actually been shot down over Dunkirk and managed to hitch a lift back on one of the 'little ships' felt that Douglas's attitude was a bit rich coming from someone who was yet to come face to face with the enemy.

222 Squadron's first contact with the enemy was to come on the afternoon of 1st June. In a fierce operation along with three other squadrons four of 222 Squadron's Hurricanes were shot down. Pilot Officer Falkust was unlucky enough to be captured and saw out the rest of the war as a POW. Sadly Pilot Officer Massey-Sharpe and Sergeant White were both killed, while Pilot Officer Roy Morant managed to force-land on the beach just over the Belgian border, after a combat with a Bf 109.

Douglas, however, was elated to have been in action and initially claimed "five for certain". Over-claiming was very easy in the height of battle and Douglas often seemed to be a little optimistic with his success rates. Eventually he was credited with one Bf 109 destroyed and one Bf 110 damaged.

Roy Morant saw the waiting soldiers scatter as he headed for the beach to make his crash landing. Fortunately he didn't hit anyone, but he saw a lot of rifles being pointed in his direction. He narrowly escaped being shot after being mistaken for a German.

The beach was being repeatedly bombed and he decided that it would be a good idea to find a tin hat. There were a lot of dead guardsmen lying there and it was suggested that he took one of their helmets, but he thought that was too callous, so he found a Belgian one that fitted.

He described how he sat in an old car with a 20-year-old platoon commander and watched the events that were taking place out in the Channel about half a mile away from where they sat. "It was just like watching a film in the comfort of a car." Destroyers were coming near to the shore to take off troops and then dive-bombers would come and disable the destroyers. Heinkels and Dorniers would follow this up with heavy bombs.

Robert Standford Tuck photographed in the cockpit of his Hurricane in autumn 1940. Tuck was an outstandingly successful fighter pilot and squadron commander who shared many of Bader's views, although the two men did not get on very well.

Earlier on they had made a number of unsuccessful attempts to reach one of the destroyers and they watched horrified when after it was disabled by dive-bombers, it was hit by a big bomb amidships and it just disappeared. They felt very lucky that they had not managed to reach it after all.

Eventually they were told to move along the coast to Dunkirk, where Roy Morant said that he had never seen such shambles, with burning buildings and burning vehicles, hastily dug graves marked by upturned rifles pushed into the ground and many bodies still unburied. Littered around was equipment of every imaginable type having simply been abandoned.

Eventually he managed to board a cross-Channel ferry and once every inch of deck space was full of people, the ship gingerly began to pick its way around sunken shipping and make its way out into the open Channel, taking a circuitous route that avoided the minefields.

Finally, with much relief he got into Folkestone at about 6.30 pm. He was directed to a train that took him to Aldershot, where he was given a meal and treated to a hot bath before being transferred to Farnborough for a flight back to Hornchurch.

He found it quite an experience to see at first hand what it was like to be down on the beach. He knew all too well that the RAF were very much in evidence, but from down below it seemed that they were never there when most wanted. Roy Morant survived the war and stayed in the RAF, rising to the rank of Group Captain. He died at his home in New South Wales at the age of 69 in August 1988.

Further patrols followed for 222 Squadron, with the last on 4th June. Douglas was now even more certain about his tactical thinking, especially following the loss of his good friend Geoffrey. To him there was no doubt that his three basic principles were unquestionably sound:

1 - he who has the height controls the battle;

2 - he who has the sun achieves surprise;

3 - he who goes in close shoots them down.

He was even more convinced that the old tactics were simply no longer appropriate.

Douglas of course was not alone in questioning official tactics and other pilots were developing similar guidance and instruction. Adolph 'Sailor' Malan had started pushing 74 Squadron patrols up to between 20,000 and 24,000 feet to avoid getting bounced over the beaches by Bf 109s.

Malan's famous Ten Rules For Air Fighting later found a place on the wall of just about every fighter station in the country.

1 - Wait until you see the whites of his eyes. Fire short bursts of one or two seconds only when your sights are definitely 'ON'.

2 - Whilst shooting think of nothing else, brace the whole of your body: have both hands on the stick: concentrate on your ring sight.

3 - Always keep a sharp lookout. "Keep your finger out."

4 - Height gives you the initiative.

5 - Always turn and face the attack.

6 - Make your decisions promptly. It is better to act quickly even though your tactics are not the best.

7 - Never fly straight and level in the combat area for more than 30 seconds.

8 - When diving to attack always leave a proportion of your formation above to act as top guard.

9 - INITIATIVE, AGGRESSION, AIR DISCIPLINE and TEAMWORK are words that MEAN something in Air Fighting.

10 - Go in quickly – Punch hard – Get out!

Other pilots like Tuck and Deere were also advocating radical changes with respect to section formations and gun harmonisation ranges. All of this was based on experience in battle.

During the Dunkirk evacuation, known as Operation Dynamo, it had been quite normal for the fighter pilots to complete three sorties in a day, but by 4th June the last troops had been brought to safety and it was essentially all over. As 222 Squadron took part in one last patrol over the port Tim Vigors looked down and described the burning fuel stores and vast clouds of smoke billowing into the air as being like something from Dante's Inferno.

By 5th June Fighter Command had lost 106 fighters over Dunkirk and over 80 pilots had been killed. Of the 261 Hurricanes that had been dispatched to fly from French airfields, only 66 returned and many of these were so badly damaged that they had to be scrapped. For Dowding these were all very worrying losses.

When 222 Squadron finally left Hornchurch on 5th June, it didn't return to Duxford, but headed off for a new home at Kirton-in-Lindsey, sixteen miles south of Lincoln.

At Kirton-in-Lindsey the Squadron was detailed to try to intercept night raiders and Douglas devised a drill that enabled his flight to scramble in 2 minutes 50 seconds - far quicker than any other flight. Tim Vigors described how it was done.

When they were on night readiness he, Douglas and Hilary Edridge slept on three camp beds at dispersal. Douglas's Spitfire was parked outside the door. Douglas liked to remove his legs when he went to sleep, so Tim was given charge of the right leg and Hilary given charge of the left one.

When the alarm sounded Tim had the responsibility of placing the right leg on Douglas's thigh, while Hilary was attending to the left leg. At the same time the two riggers who were responsible for Douglas's aircraft would have rushed in and grabbing him under the arms would carry him bodily out to his aircraft and lift him onto the wing. Douglas would then grab the sides of the cockpit and leaver himself into his seat. Tim and Hilary meanwhile would be sprinting to their own Spitfires. With Douglas in front, the three would then taxi to the big floodlight that marked the take-off area.

Late in the evening of 12th June Douglas had a mishap and seriously damaged another Spitfire. He was coming into land after a night patrol when according to his CO his approach was far too high and too fast. He skidded off the flare path and crashed into a hedge. Douglas was furious and initially was loath to admit responsibility, blaming the layout of the flare path. His CO had a different view and put the reason for the accident as 'sheer bad flying'.

Although Douglas feared that he might be grounded, eleven days later Mermagen officially rated him as 'exceptional' and 'quite an outstanding personality'.

Events move quickly in wartime and Douglas was not to stay with 222 Squadron for very much longer. Not long after Douglas and 222 Squadron had moved up to Kirton-in-Lindsey, Woody had a phone call from Leigh-Mallory telling him that 242 (Canadian) Squadron were reporting to Coltishall and would be under the control of Duxford.

242 Squadron had had a very tough time in France. Casualties had been high and they had literally had to move from field to field. The squadron adjutant, Peter MacDonald MP, had managed to evacuate the ground crews via Cherbourg, but all tools, spares, kit and baggage had to be abandoned. The squadron's CO had left the pilots to their own devices and they had flown to Coltishall under the direction of Flying Officer Stan Taylor, but the pilots had arrived with nothing other than the clothes they were wearing.

"I've got to find them a new squadron commander," Leigh-Mallory told Woody. "He's got to be good because these chaps are Canadians and have had a rough time and they're browned off with authority and need a good leader - any suggestions?"

Woody immediately suggested Douglas.

"I thought you would say that," was the response. "I think you are right."

Leigh-Mallory sent for Douglas to personally tell him that he was giving him a squadron of his own. This was to take immediate effect. The date was 24th June 1940, about 4½ months after he had re-joined the RAF through the main gate of RAF Duxford.

Squadron Leader

To say that 242 Squadron was demoralised would be serious understatement. 242 was a Canadian squadron that had been formed the previous year using some of the many Canadian officers who were serving with the RAF. The CO had been appointed by the Canadian government in Ottawa, but this had been a disastrous choice since the unfortunate man had come direct from Training Command and had no operational experience. He then found himself pitched into the thick of the chaotic attempts to stem the German invasion of France.

As the French armies had fallen back, the squadron was forced to withdraw, and withdraw again, and again until it was almost at Saint-Nazaire. By now the squadron was in tatters, with many pilots having been killed. The CO was at the end of his tether and in no fit state to lead and the squadron had become separated from its ground crews with the remaining pilots now having to service their own aircraft.

The adjutant had also become separated from the aircrew and was busy trying to round up the ground personnel who were somewhere in the region of Le Mans, racing towards the coast ahead of the advancing Germans. It was decided that there was nowhere else to go, but back to England, so they flew to Tangmere and then on to Coltishall.

Leigh-Mallory flew himself down to Coltishall to meet hem. He was shocked by what he saw. He was the first contact that the squadron had had with any sort of authority for weeks and he listened to them intently. There was no commanding officer and no proper flight commanders. The most senior officer present appeared to be a Canadian Pilot Officer called Stan Turner.

Turner later went on to serve with great distinction and rose to the rank of Group Captain by the end of the war, but he could be obstinate and rebellious if provoked and was both blunt and direct in expressing his views to the AOC. Leigh-Mallory listened carefully and it rapidly became clear to that an exceptional man was needed to fill the post of CO for 242 Squadron. He thought that he knew just who that man could be and was happy that Woody had agreed with his choice. However, since 242 was a Canadian squadron, the appointment would need to be cleared by the Canadian government representatives in London.

Douglas was now aged 30 and considered to be rather old for a fighter pilot since the C-in-C of Fighter Command, Air Chief Marshall Sir Hugh Dowding, was of the opinion that the upper age for commanders of fighter squadrons should be 26.

Douglas was summoned to Leigh-Mallory's HQ at Hucknall. He was concerned that mention might be made of his unfortunate crash twelve days earlier, but the AOC brushed this aside and went straight into the real reasons for his wanting to see him.

After a long talk with the AOC, Douglas was left with no illusions as to the major task that lay ahead of him. It was the third week of June 1940 and the entire European coast from northern Holland right down to the Brest peninsula and beyond was now occupied by the enemy. With the French airfields in German hands, aerial attacks inevitably would soon

A formation of 9 Hurricanes over England in 1940. The official RAF tactical handbook favoured this sort of tightly grouped formation in combat, but Bader's experience of combat caused him to argue for looser formations.

A German Heinkel He111 bomber over the East End of London during the Battle of Britain. The He111 was the Luftwaffe's standard bomber during the early stages of war and was able to carry over two tons of bombs.

begin as part of a softening up process before the anticipated invasion. Douglas realised that he might have a fortnight, but certainly no more, to get his new squadron into shape as a potent and disciplined force.

He knew that the first job was to get things right on the ground - getting things right in the air would then follow. There were key positions that had to be filled, such as the two flight commanders, the adjutant, the engineering officer and the senior NCOs.

He decided that fresh blood was needed for the flight commanders and his first choices were Tim Vigors and Hilary Edridge, but after due consideration they both decided to stay with 222 Squadron. Hilary Edridge's comment was: "That mad bugger will get us all killed when the real war starts!"

As fate would have it, Hilary only had about three more months left to live. On 30th October 1940, following combat with some Bf 109s he sustained a head injury and although he managed to crash land his badly damaged Spitfire near Ewhurst in Surrey, the aircraft turned over and caught fire. He was pulled from the wreckage and taken to hospital where he died from his wounds later that day. He was later buried close to his parents' home near Bath.

His great friend Tim Vigors survived to served with distinction in the Far East, ending the war as a wing commander. The title of Tim's autobiography summed up the general feeling of the time: Life's too short to cry.

For his flight commanders Douglas chose Eric Ball from 19 Squadron and George Powell-Sheldon who was recommended by 12 Group HQ. He decided to stick with Flight Lieutenant Peter MacDonald as adjutant. MacDonald was a Canadian, but he had been an undergraduate at Cambridge during the Great War. He had established contacts with the Hudson Bay Company and had entered the House of Commons in 1924 as MP for the Isle of Wight.

He knew his way around the corridors of power and his sixteen years in parliament had given him status, influence and access to ministers. True, he liked his drink, which was why he was usually known in the squadron as 'Boozy Mac', but underneath, Douglas recognised a man with shrewd political judgement who apart from everything else knew all about Canada and the Canadians.

His first meeting with the pilots was not a success. Accompanied by the adjutant he went to inspect them in the dispersal hut where they were lounging around reading comics. For a start the sullen Canadians refused to stand when he entered, but simply lowered their comics to look at him over their tops. When the pilots didn't seem to like what they saw, they raised them up again and carried on reading.

Douglas was furious and got the adjutant to assemble the pilots for what he described as a "three-minute talk on dress and deportment". When he finished his tirade he asked if anyone had anything to say. Pilot Officer Stan Turner looked him in the eye and said: "Horse-shit!" There was a long pause before he added: "Sir".

Douglas said nothing, but stumped out, climbed into a Hurricane and proceeded to spend the next half-hour demonstrating his skill at Hendon-style aerobatics. By the time that he landed the Canadians had come to realise that there was more to their new CO than they had originally thought.

RAF ground crew prepare to load belts of .303 machine gun ammunition into a Hurricane fighter. Bader was an outspoken proponent of the advantages of quick firing machine guns in combat over the slower cannon being introduced in 1941.

Once he was made aware that his pilots had lost much of their uniform kit in France he apologised for his remarks about their scruffy appearance, but insisted that they should dress like officers and gentlemen, particularly in the mess. He said that they should borrow where possible, but he would ensure that funds were available if they were to go into Norwich and order missing things from local tailors.

Almost immediately training began in earnest.

Warrant Officer Bernard West had been engineering officer of 242 and Douglas decided to keep him. He sensed that Mr West, as he always called him, would be the linchpin and indispensable prop on which to build. West on the other hand knew that the relationship with his squadron commander must be based on total understanding and regard. In the same way that to Douglas his metal legs were something of an irrelevance, to Mr West the important things about Douglas were his attitude and his service credentials.

Bernard West was fiercely loyal to his squadron and he knew that somebody was going to have to sort it out and establish morale. He realised that Douglas would be an exacting and uncompromising commander, but was prepared to support him 250%. Something that Mr West realised from the start was that there would be big trouble if he didn't get 242's aircraft strength and serviceability on the top line,

The problems were immediate. The squadron had eighteen brand new Hurricane MkIs on its strength, but no spare parts and no proper sets of tools to work with. When Mr West reported this situation to Douglas the reaction was just as he predicted that it would be. In modern parlance Douglas "went ballistic".

He sent off the now famous signal to group headquarters, with a copy to Fighter Command HQ: "242 Squadron now operational as regards pilots but non-operational, repeat, non-operational as regards equipment."

It was only after he had sent the signals that he told his outraged station commander what he had done. Normal practice would have been to ask another squadron to lend a hand, but Douglas was not like that. This was his squadron and as far as he was concerned his needs were more important than any other squadron that might be waiting further up the line.

The response from Fighter Command came the same day. A squadron leader in charge of equipment phoned to argue that there were shortages in many units and 242 ought to borrow what was needed from other squadrons. Something of a shouting match developed that resulted in both phones being slammed down.

The AOC flew down to Coltishall to try and smooth things over and agreed to see what could be done. Before anything could be done Douglas received a summons to Fighter Command HQ at Bentley Priory for an interview with the C-in-C himself, Air Chief Marshall Sir Hugh Dowding.

This could have meant the end of a promising career for Douglas, but although the C-in-C made it clear that he did not think much of Douglas's signal, what really irked him was the supply officer's assertion that he, Dowding, would be furious at what Douglas had done. Dowding did not take kindly to other people predicting how he would or would not react, least of all a comparatively junior officer.

The outcome was that the offending squadron leader lost his job at Fighter Command, as did the station equipment officer at Coltishall. 242 Squadron received its requested equipment within 48 hours and became fully operational on 9th July 1940.

Needless to say, Mr West was delighted and the pilots were now beginning to understand that they had acquired a CO who really got things moving.

Douglas now set about applying all his skills and flair to pulling the squadron together in the air. Pilot Officer Denis Crowley-Milling remembered vividly the impact that the new CO had on the pilots.

No one ever thought of questioning his authority or challenging his tactics; nor did any of the younger members risk stepping out of line. Behind all the ribaldry, laughter and bravado, there lay an iron discipline. The Canadians were something of a maverick lot and they had found difficulty in accepting the rulebook, but they recognised very quickly that there was only one voice that counted in 242 Squadron.

Aerobatics and simulated combat became second nature. Douglas also made the squadron go through as many movements as he could together. One aim was to make the pilots feel that they were part of a group and not simply a number of individuals. The other was to instil tightness, discipline and control to their flying.

A group of RAF pilots inspect the wreckage of a downed German bomber. Pilots were keen trophy hunters eager to make off with bent propellers, tail fins and other relics with which to decorate their rooms and airfields.

From 9th July onwards enemy raiders began to attack the East Coast and 242 Squadron were fully operational both day and night. The official start of the Battle of Britain is given as 19th July, although many regard the true start as being back in May with the Dunkirk evacuation.

The German invasion was code named Operation Sea Lion and the Luftwaffe had been set the task of achieving air superiority prior to this. This air superiority was vital to ensure the safety of the vast armada of slow-moving river barges and other craft that were to transport the invading troops across the Channel.

Head of the Luftwaffe, Reich Marshal Herman Göring was full of confidence. He believed that his "boys" were invincible and saw beating the RAF as being no problem. The RAF would be cleared from the skies and the invasion could take place on the day for which it had been planned.

For the time being the Coltishall squadrons had to be content with rather tedious North Sea patrols interspersed with occasional bursts of action. Douglas managed to add to his total of 'kills' on 11th July when in very poor weather he managed to intercept and shoot down a Dornier Do 17 that crashed into the sea off Cromer, with no survivors.

With their easy access to Southern England from the newly acquired French airfields the Luftwaffe began to show increased activity and before long the Battle of Britain really began to get underway. The squadrons of 11 Group in southeast England were soon heavily engaged, but 242 Squadron, being part of 12 Group was kept in reserve, only to be called upon when particularly needed.

The two Coltishall squadrons, 242 and 66, were becoming increasingly frustrated at not being called upon to take part. The shipping lanes of the North Sea still needed to be patrolled and it was during this time that Douglas and his friend Rupert Leigh, CO of 66 Squadron, first began to experiment flying both of their squadrons together. What began as a way of filling in time while they waited for the call for action, effectively became the early trials of what developed into the famous Duxford Big Wing that was later to prove so controversial.

In the Thick of It

On Friday 30th August 242 Squadron finally got the call for action. The day broke with fair weather stretching from North Norfolk as far as the other side of the English Channel. As day broke, the rising sun slowly warmed up the Hurricanes of 242 Squadron that had been dispersed around the airfield at RAF Coltishall.

Douglas had always been a light sleeper and was already awake when his batman, Stokoe, tapped on his door just before 6.00 am with his morning tea. Stokoe left it near the pair of artificial legs and departed. Douglas was immediately out of bed, made his way to the adjoining bathroom on his hands, had a bath and a shave and then moved back to his bedroom where he strapped on his legs and put on his uniform. By 6.25 he was in the mess having a light breakfast of toast, butter and marmalade.

Soon after half past six the phone rang and it was a call for the squadron to fly down to Duxford for possible action at last. The eager pilots took off and headed south, but after about ten or twelve minutes they got a call to return to Coltishall. Douglas was understandably furious, but not much more than an hour after they had returned the phone rang again and it was another call to go to Duxford. Shortly after 9.00 am the 12 Hurricanes of 242 Squadron set off once again for the 25-minute flight and this time they were not recalled.

When they arrived at Duxford everything was very quiet. Douglas immediately asked Woody: "What's the form?" and all Woody could reply was: "Nothing at the moment." All through the morning and into the afternoon the pilots of 242 Squadron received reports of Luftwaffe intruders bombing RAF airfields in the southeast; including Biggin Hill,

A Spitfire cruises through the skies in front of the White Cliffs of Dover. The Battle of Britain was fought for control of the air over the English Channel for without it the Germans did not dare launch their invasion fleet to attack Britain.

Tangmere, Shoreham and Kenley. They knew that squadrons from 11 Group were heavily engaged, but still no call came to them.

Douglas was deeply frustrated at all this hanging around and by about 4 o'clock a good number of the pilots were thinking that they would soon be receiving the call to return to Coltishall.

As Douglas fretted and fumed, suddenly at 4.45 pm the phone rang to call them to fly down to North Weald, just south of Duxford.

Keith Park, the AOC of 11 Group had all his squadrons committed and since a fresh wave of German bombers was approaching he wanted a 12 Group squadron to protect North Weald. Once he was airborne Douglas called Duxford operations and spoke to Woody who told him that seventy-plus 'bandits' were approaching North Weald at 15,000 feet.

Douglas calculated that if he stuck to the heading he had been given and if the enemy were where they were supposed to be, by the time that he arrived the enemy would have the sun behind them and be difficult to spot. He decided to steer another 30 degrees west, but when he arrived there was no sign of the enemy.

One of his flight commanders spotted some unidentified aircraft in the distance and Douglas sent George Powell-Sheldon's Blue Section to investigate. He was now left with ten Hurricanes, counting his own. Suddenly, just west of Enfield they encountered a huge enemy force flying eastwards. Douglas counted fourteen blocks of six bombers, with thirty Bf 110 fighters behind and above. They were ten against more than a hundred.

Douglas led the attack and the fighting was fierce. The battle lasted for between five and ten minutes, but suddenly the enemy scattered and the sky cleared. The jubilant 242 Squadron returned to Duxford claiming 12 victories and three probables. Although later investigation put the true number of those destroyed as only four, this did not detract from their elation. None of the Hurricanes was damaged.

They flew back to Coltishall in the gathering dusk. It had been a funny sort of day with an awful lot of waiting around, but as they all agreed there was a very worthwhile ending to what had otherwise been a very tedious day.

Douglas received congratulatory messages from Leigh-Mallory, the Chief of Air Staff and the Under-Secretary of State for Air. Later, at Duxford, Douglas expounded at some length to Woody his view that the one who was in command in the sky should be the one to decide the height and direction of attack, rather than the controller on the ground

At Leigh-Mallory's request he later wrote up the battle in the form of a memo for the station commander at Coltishall. In it he recommended that if 11 Group wished to score the same kind of success and suffer lower casualties than had hitherto been the case, his tactics should be employed in future. In view of the fact that 11 Group had been meeting large enemy formations on a day-to-day basis for some time and 242 Squadron had only met such a formation just once, this all seemed rather presumptuous, but that was typically Douglas.

When Leigh-Mallory congratulated Douglas in person, Douglas was not shy to put forward the view that if he had had three squadrons of 36 or more planes at his disposal instead of 12, he could have shot down three times as many.

Leigh-Mallory liked this. It gave him ammunition that might prove useful in a power struggle that was brewing between him and Keith Park, his opposite number at 11 Group.

In the late 1930s, following the increase in German military might there was a perceived threat of a possible invasion. If such an invasion were to come, the accepted view was that it would take place in Eastern England along the North Sea coast. This seemed to be the logical area, where the terrain was fairly flat and there were plenty of suitable landing sites for the airborne troops that were expected to mount the attack.

The expectation was that the invaders would aim to gain a foothold and once this had been achieved, a two-pronged attack would be relatively easy with one group of the enemy sweeping across to the industrial

A member of the Royal Observer Corps scans the skies over London. In 1940 radar was ineffective over land, so Bader and other fighter pilots were reliant on reports from spotters such as this to locate enemy aircraft.

Midlands and up into the north of England, while the other swung south to encircle London. The RAF's defensive tactics were all based on this presumption.

Never in anyone's wildest dreams was it ever considered that France would fall and bring Britain within range of enemy fighters.

The drawing up of Britain's aerial defence plan, had been the responsibility of Hugh Dowding, Fighter Command's C-in-C, together with Keith Park, who at the time was Dowding's senior staff officer. The plan divided the country up into Fighter Groups, which in turn were divided into sectors, with each sector controlling individual squadrons that were based at main or satellite airfields.

Air Vice Marshal Keith Park commanded 11 Group during the Battle of Britain. Bader opposed his tactic of using fighter squadrons individually, instead preferring "Big Wings" of aircraft.

Observations from the Observer Corps and radar stations would be collected and assessed at Fighter Command HQ and forwarded to the appropriate Group operations room. This would enable a picture to be built up of the size and direction of incoming raids and enable the appropriate number of squadrons to be dispatched to meet them.

Since all RAF tactics were based on meeting forces of enemy bombers over the North Sea, this would place the airfields of 12 Group under the command of Leigh-Mallory at the forefront of the defence of the realm.

It actually didn't happen this way because France did fall and when the bomber forces began attacking the southeast they were supported by large numbers of fighters. Hence it was the squadrons of 11 Group under the leadership of Keith Park who were getting all the action, rather than those of Leigh-Mallory.

Park believed that the situation in 11 Group was best suited to the plan where individual squadrons would be used as interceptors and that in this way he was often managing to break up large bomber formations before they reached their targets and he was also inflicting heavier losses on the enemy than the RAF was sustaining. He believed that 11 Group's situation did not lend itself to the assembly of large forces, considering that this simply took up too much time and would allow the enemy to reach and bomb the target.

Those in favour of larger forces maintained that the prime purpose was to shoot down as many enemy aircraft as possible and this was best done by using large numbers of fighters. The high losses that the enemy would sustain as a result would cause the raids to diminish, or stop altogether. In other words it didn't really matter if you didn't catch the enemy before he reached the target because you could get him on the way home.

There had also been criticism in some quarters that often squadrons or even flights had been hopelessly outnumbered when they were sent up to intercept groups of incoming enemy aircraft.

A further argument against using a large force was that even if the force could get off the ground quickly, which was not always the case, three squadrons being controlled as one were less likely to spot an intended raid than three squadrons being controlled separately, simply because there was a lot of sky over southern England where the enemy could operate.

As the controversy developed, views became polarised and criticism began to be levelled at the way that Fighter Command had conducted the battle. It was obviously very easy for those who were not running things to be critical of those who were.

Civilians eagerly gaze at a downed Messerschmitt Bf109 near Dover during the Battle of Britain. Wrecks such as this were taken away to be studied by RAF "boffins" - scientists looking for new developments in the enemy's aircraft.

As is well documented, by following Dowding's squadron-based system Park used 11 Group's 20 squadrons to fight the Battle of Britain with great skill. However, many writers and pilots have accepted that there should have been better coordination between 11 Group and 12 Group. This was especially apparent when incoming raids overlapped the territory of both groups.

The growing scale of the Luftwaffe attacks, coupled with Leigh-Mallory's frustration that his squadrons were not being used, allowed the proponents of mass fighter formations to ultimately gain ascendancy.

Early in September Leigh-Mallory gave Douglas the green light to try operating 242, 19 and 310 squadrons from Duxford as a single tactical unit. 242's Hurricanes moved down to Duxford from Coltishall to join 310 Squadron, while 19 Squadron stayed at RAF Foulmere, Duxford's satellite station about three miles away.

310 was comprised mainly of Czechoslovakian pilots who had escaped from their own country to join the French Air Force and then escaped for a second time after the fall of France. The squadron had joint COs, Squadron Leader Douglas Blackwood and Squadron Leader Sasha Hess. It also had two British Flight Commanders.

Alexander (Sasha) Hess was about 45, so a good bit older than the other pilots. He was quite famous in Czech air circles and had been leader of the Czech aerobatic team in European air displays during the 1930s. It was after he escaped that he learnt that his wife and daughter had perished in a concentration camp. This led to him having a deep hatred for all Germans and he vowed that he would never show any mercy or take any prisoners.

The first occasion the Czech squadron went into action he shot down a German bomber and saw the three crew members scramble out with their hands up. He later told Woody: "I hesitate, then it was too late, so I go round again to make sure I kill them; they wave something white; again I did not shoot them. I think it is no use; I am become too bloody British!"

There was no question as to who would lead the Wing since Douglas was the most senior and most forceful of the three squadron leaders. Flight Lieutenant Gordon Sinclair had transferred from 19 Squadron to become one of the two British flight commanders of 310 Squadron. His comment was: "we just automatically assumed that Douglas would lead".

Douglas Blackwood, CO of 310 Squadron, said: "We never did any practice sorties as a Wing. We just went off on an operational patrol together one day with Douglas leading".

Saturday 7th September was the day when the Wing scored its first and very spectacular success. Thirteen days earlier, on Sunday 25th August, due to what was said to have been a navigational error, a German plane had dropped some bombs on London. This was against strict orders, but the RAF had immediately taken up the challenge and mounted a number of raids over Berlin.

Göring and Hitler were humiliated. They had always maintained that no attack on Berlin would be possible and as a result Göring took personal control of an assault on London. Every available aircraft was to be used, with more bombers than ever before.

Just before 4.00 pm the first reports started to come through that a raid was pending and 11 Group was alerted. A vast formation of aircraft, 20 miles wide and a mile and a half high, was stacked in layers from 14,000 feet to 20,000 feet. There were 348 bombers and 617 fighters.

At 17 minutes past 4, the first eleven fighter squadrons of 11 Group were scrambled and six minutes later the remaining squadrons in the Group were brought to readiness. By 4.30 every squadron in the London area was airborne, bringing the total to 23.

Prior to this the airfields had been the Luftwaffe's major targets and Dowding knew that if this was again the plan, it was almost certain that the RAF would be completely wiped out, allowing the enemy complete domination of the skies and making an invasion a certainty rather than just a possibility.

Very soon it became clear that this was to be no ordinary raid. Once the enemy aircraft had crossed the coast they started changing direction, criss-crossing flight paths and making it very difficult to interpret their intentions. It gradually became clear that it was not the airfields that were the targets, but that the target was actually London. This was confirmed when the first of three separate waves hit the East End.

Since the expected targets had been the airfields, the 23 squadrons were all in the wrong place and only a few were able to intercept the bombers before they reached the city. As usual Douglas was raring to go, but had to wait for the call from 11 Group. This came at 4.45 pm and the Duxford Wing took off and headed south towards North Weald, a little less than 15 minutes flying time away.

Their information was that the enemy would be approaching from the east at a height of 10,000 feet, but when the Duxford aircraft arrived, they found the enemy to be 10,000 feet higher than this. This would mean that the RAF would have no height advantage and would be attacking bombers with fighters above them and in the eye of the sun.

Douglas was angry that the Wing had not been scrambled earlier because that would have given the pilots the chance to gain more height. He decided that rather than head for Maidstone as he had been directed, he led the Wing in the direction of the Isle of Sheppey. Consequently most of the fighting took place over the Thames Estuary and it was fast and furious.

As the Hurricanes were climbing they got 'bounced' by about 60 Bf 109s. Douglas's Hurricane was badly damaged and Sub-Lieutenant Dickie Cork, a Fleet Air Arm pilot attached to 242 Squadron was slightly injured. 25-year-old Pilot Officer John Benzie, one of 242's Canadian pilots whose home was in Winnipeg, disappeared without trace. It is assumed that he crashed into the Estuary. He is commemorated at the RAF Memorial at Runnymede among those who have no known grave. 310 Squadron also lost two of its Hurricanes. Both pilots survived, although one was grievously burned.

When the squadrons landed, about an hour after they had originally taken off, the final tally for 242 Squadron was 10 confirmed destroyed, with 2 probables and 3 damaged; 310 Squadron destroyed 5, with 3 probables and 3 damaged, while the Spitfires of 19 Squadron destroyed a further 5 of the enemy.

A flight of Spitfires in the air "somewhere over England". The openings of the machine gun ports in the leading edge of the wings can be clearly seen.

A Messerchmitt Bf109, the most effective German fighter in 1940. The Germans closely guarded the designs of their aircraft and it was not until early in 1940 when one was shot down that the British realised this aircraft was armed with both machine guns and cannon.

Although the figures were later revealed to have been grossly over-estimated, at the time the action was considered to be a great success and congratulatory messages poured in.

Douglas, however was furious that the Wing had not been scrambled earlier, pointing out that if they had been scrambled before the enemy crossed the Channel, the RAF pilots would have had time to get into a position of tactical superiority.

On 9th September the Luftwaffe repeated what it had done two days previously and just after 4.00 pm sent over two waves in quick succession. Late in the afternoon the Duxford Wing was scrambled and told to patrol over North Weald and Hornchurch at 20,000 feet.

Once he was airborne Douglas climbed to 22,000 feet and headed for Staines, where at about 5.40 pm he saw a large force of enemy aircraft approximately 15 miles to the southwest. An intense air battle took place and at the end of the day 242 Squadron claimed to have destroyed 11 of the enemy; 310 Squadron destroyed 3 with 3 probables and 1 damaged; and 19 Squadron's tally was 6 destroyed, 1 probable and 1 damaged.

This was not without cost. Two of 19 Squadron's Spitfires were damaged and 242 lost two of its Hurricanes. Although Sgt R W Lonsdale parachuted to safety, Pilot Officer Kirkpatrick, one of the Canadian pilots died after crash landing his Hurricane near Rye.

310 Squadron lost three of its Hurricanes. Pilot Officer Rypl crash landed but was unhurt, while Flying Officer Gordon Sinclair and Pilot Officer John Boulton, together with a German pilot were involved in what was said to be the biggest mid-air collision in the Battle of Britain.

Only Gordon Sinclair survived the collision and since it took place at an altitude of somewhere around 20,000, his parachute descent lasted for nearly 13 minutes. He landed in a wood near Coulsden in Surrey, where the first person on the scene chanced to be an old school friend who was now an officer in the Irish Guards. Sinclair was invited back to the Guards' Depot at Caterham to dine, but he was refused admittance on the grounds that he was improperly dressed. It had been an early start and Sinclair was wearing his flying clothes on top of his pyjamas.

He had also come out without any money and it is said that he had great difficulty in borrowing enough for his train fare back to Duxford.

Once again Douglas had disobeyed instructions. As Air Vice-Marshall 'Johnnie' Johnson later commented: "fortunately for Bader neither North Weald nor Hornchurch was attacked, otherwise Park might have lodged an official complaint with Dowding".

In spite of this, the end seemed to justify the means. 20 aircraft destroyed was a good number. It may not have been accurate, but it enabled political capital to be made and that was considered to be important. The following day Douglas flew up to 12 Group HQ to discuss the Wing's progress to date with Leigh-Mallory.

Leigh-Mallory showed his delight by offering Douglas two more squadrons, 302 (Polish) Squadron and 611 Squadron, to add to his Wing. It had also been informally approved that Douglas could interpret instructions from the ground as he saw fit.

The first time the five squadrons of the extended Big Wing flew together was late in the afternoon of 14th September. 242, 310 and 302 Squadrons flew Hurricanes, while the other two squadrons flew Spitfires. As before they patrolled the area around North Weald and Hornchurch, but they saw no action. It was to be rather different the following day.

The Power Struggle

On Sunday 15th September, although nobody knew it at the time, this was to be the defining day of the Battle of Britain. The early mist slowly cleared and although the light cumulus cloud was enough to produce a little rain in places, visibility remained good, with a gentle westerly wind that moved round to northwest as the day advanced.

At around 11.30 Göring launched the first wave of his morning attack of 100 or so aircraft, shortly to be followed by a further 150. It was a formidable force made up of Dornier Do 17s and Do 215s, escorted by Messerschmitt Bf 109s. They were flying at various heights between 15,000 feet and 26,000 feet.

Defenders were scrambled and for about 45 minutes a fierce battle raged over east Kent and London. Even so, about 100 enemy bombers reached south and east London, with some actually being intercepted over the centre. Sixteen squadrons of 11 Group were initially involved, closely followed by five squadrons from 12 Group. Squadrons from 10 Group were also called in.

242 Squadron was ordered off from Coltishall at precisely 11.22 and flew down to Duxford, where according to the plan, they formed up with 310, 302, 19 and 611 Squadrons and headed south towards the action. For once the timing was right and they were in an ideal position with respect to height and the position of the sun.

Douglas led the Wing to patrol a flexible area over Gravesend. The three Hurricane squadrons, 242, 310 and 302 flew at around 25,000 feet, ready to meet the bombers, while the two Spitfire squadrons, 10 and 611, were a bit higher at between 26,000 and 27,000 feet, ready to deal with the fighters.

In a space between noon and 12.30, a total of between 150 and 200 individual combats took place in an area of sky roughly 8 miles long, 38 miles broad and between 4 and 6 miles high.

It has to be remembered these combats often took place at speeds of between 300 and 400 miles an hour. An enemy plane might have been intercepted over Hammersmith and destroyed over Dungeness. Many combats went as far as the French coast. Sgt J A Potter of 19 Squadron was involved in just such a chase, but unfortunately for him, having got that far he was shot down and ended up as a POW.

Douglas later commented that: "at one time you could see planes all over the place and the sky seemed full of parachutes. It was sudden death that morning for our fighters shot them to blazes".

The 56 fighters of the Duxford Wing returned to base having claimed a total of 26 enemy aircraft destroyed, plus 8 probables and 2 damaged. There was hardly time to get their aircraft refuelled and grab a quick sandwich before they were ordered off again at 12 minutes past 2. Although the same five squadrons were involved, this time there were only 49 fighters rather than 56.

By now the sky was covered by eight-tenths cloud at 5,000 feet, but Douglas led the aircraft through a gap in the cloud and hurried south

William Sholto Douglas was Assistant Chief of the Air Staff in 1940 and so one of the most influential non-combat officers. His support for Bader's "Big Wing" tactic proved to be decisive in the on-going disputes.

towards North Weald, still climbing. Before long they sighted the enemy formation, but they saw to their dismay that they were about three or four thousand feet below the Luftwaffe formations. Not only did the Wing have no height advantage, but its aircraft were badly positioned with respect to the sun. Douglas was furious that they had not been scrambled ten minutes earlier.

Once again the fighting was fierce, with dogfights stretching from London as far as Maidstone. On their return to Duxford the Wing claimed a further 26 aircraft destroyed, with 8 probables and 1 damaged. In 2 sorties that day the Wing had amassed a total of 52 confirmed kills, which formed a significant proportion of the 185 kills that Fighter Command had confirmed for the day.

Once again these figures had been wildly optimistic since the actual true number of enemy aircraft destroyed that day was only 56. Leigh-Mallory obviously did not know this when he wrote his glowing congratulations.

While Douglas was happy with the number of aircraft that had been shot down by the Duxford Wing, he was not at all happy with the way things had gone during the afternoon. In his usual dogmatic way he forcibly expressed to the AOC that he felt let down in that the squadrons had been called into the air too late. He also complained that in his opinion the policy of letting 11 Group squadrons fight the battle, while keeping 12 Group squadrons in reserve, was fundamentally flawed.

Douglas's theory was that as soon as the Luftwaffe began to assemble on the other side of the Channel, the 12 Group squadrons should be scrambled and then head south. This would enable the Luftwaffe to be attacked while 11 Group squadrons were getting off the ground and gaining height.

This was contrary to Fighter Command's established and carefully thought-out plan, but Douglas saw his Big Wing theory as being complementary to the squadrons of 11 Group rather than in opposition.

In Douglas's mind there was also another important factor that needed to be taken into consideration to ensure success and as ever, he was not at all reluctant to share his opinion. Control, he felt, had to come from the centre at Fighter Command Headquarters in Stanmore rather than from Group controllers.

It was only the C-in-C who had a complete picture of what was going on. Group commanders were limited to their own areas, but incoming raids often overlapped Group boundaries. This presented problems when squadrons from one Group crossed into the territory of another. Douglas of course was not the only one to identify the flaw in the plan, but he was one of the most vocal in his criticism of it.

Dowding, however, did not see the need for a comprehensive Command control until very late on, by which time the differences between Park and Leigh-Mallory had festered to the point where they were effectively beyond redemption. In hindsight early intervention by Dowding could and should have defused the situation, but early intervention did not happen.

On 14th September 1940 Douglas was awarded the DSO.

The last big battle for the Duxford Wing occurred on 27th September. By now 302 (Polish) Squadron had left Duxford and 616 Squadron had replaced 611 Squadron. There were now four squadrons making up the Wing; 19, 242, 310 and 616 and at 11.45 am they took off and headed for the Dover-Canterbury area where they arrived about 30 minutes later.

By then the squadrons were at an altitude of about 23,000 feet and they spotted a force of Bf 109s about 3,000 to 4,000 feet below them. There was a fast and furious action during which 13 of the Messerschmitts were shot down for the loss of three British aircraft. Two of the British pilots were wounded, one of whom, Flying Office Donald Smith of 616 Squadron died the following day, but Gordon Sinclair of 310 managed to bail out unhurt after his aircraft caught fire. The time was now 12.20.

Events continued to move quickly and five minutes later a pilot from Douglas's squadron, 21-year-old Flying Officer Michael Homer DFC, was shot down and killed. The third fatality from this particular action was Pilot Officer Eric Burgoyne from 19 Squadron.

The final reckoning was 13 enemy aircraft shot down and once again Leigh-Mallory and the pilots were elated. Later a message was received from Air Vice-Marshal Park that the Duxford pilots had been poaching on 11 Group's preserves. The pilots initially thought that this was Park's way of congratulating them on their success, but they later realised that it was actually in the nature of a formal complaint for trespassing.

Shortly after this 616 Squadron returned to Yorkshire and the Wing was back to the original three squadrons, 242, 19 and 310. Things had begun to go quiet. During October the slimmed-down wing was called up on only ten occasions and managed to make just one partial contact.

By now Leigh-Mallory was making a great impression with the reports that he was widely circulating about the success of the Big Wing from Duxford and the numbers of enemy that had been shot down by it.

The true figures show that there was always a good deal of over-claiming, often by a factor of between four and seven to one. This was not due to dishonesty, but simply to the fact that with so many aircraft in the air at the same time it was not always easy to see who shot at what. It was very easy for two or three pilots to genuinely believe that he was responsible for shooting down the same aircraft.

This over-claiming was immaterial to Leigh-Mallory; these after all were confirmed claims and that's what mattered. His report, forwarded to Dowding, made it clear that in his opinion 12 Group could teach the rest of Fighter Command a thing or two about the advantages of large and offensively orientated formations.

Leigh-Mallory had good friends in the Air Ministry and soon his ideas were rumbling around the corridors of power and there was beginning to be talk that Dowding and Park had been conducting the Battle of Britain with a dangerously defensive mentality.

One of the great supporters of the Big Wing was Air Vice-Marshall Sholto Douglas, Deputy Chief of Air Staff. He made his feelings quite clear: "the best way to stop an enemy air offensive is to shoot down such

A pair of Messerschmitt Bf110 fighters. The Bf110 was designed to be a "destroyer", that is a long range interceptor and bomber escort. It proved to be vulnerable to the Spitfire and Hurricane.

a large proportion of the enemy bomber force that they are compelled to diminish the scale of their offensive, or even call it off altogether".

The 12 Group Wing was now being used as a test case for this line of thinking and consequently as a stick with which to beat Dowding and Park and force them to alter their operational approach.

A definite power struggle was getting underway for the control of Fighter Command. Dowding and Park were being squared up to by the powerful forces of Sholto Douglas and Leigh-Mallory, with their Air Ministry supporters. Dowding was already past retirement age and it was almost as though the vultures were sitting on the fence.

It is not clear how much Douglas was aware of these backroom machinations; probably very little. Even if he was aware, he probably had little concern about the developing power struggle. Douglas had very firm ideas about a number of things and was never averse to expounding on these, very forcibly and at great length to anyone who would listen to him. He was convinced that his ideas were 100% correct and to him no other idea was worth considering.

All he wanted was to see his ideas accepted and put into practice. In short, in the battle for control of Fighter Command that was to follow, Douglas may have been an important tool, but rather than being a conscious player he was really nothing more than an unwitting tool.

He was always fiercely loyal to those who had been put in authority over him. He was after all a Cranwell man and respect for seniority was very important to him. Dowding, had been very good to him when he first took command of 242 Squadron, during the time that he was struggling to equip it. The altercation that Douglas had with the supply officer was, as Douglas put it to Dowding, "a disagreement between two officers of equal rank" and Dowding had come down on his side. In fact Douglas later expressed great fondness for his gruff, withdrawn C-in-C, who sometimes appeared rather inarticulate in the company of others

Douglas's friends always agreed that he was not a particularly subtle thinker. Although he was capable of changing his mind, he was not devious and was widely regarded as being incapable of knowingly undermining people that he admired, especially father figures like Dowding.

Leigh-Mallory had a bit of a reputation in the service for picking up ideas that he liked and then passing them off as his own. He had liked Douglas's ideas and he saw them as possible ammunition in his power struggle with Keith Park, his opposite number in 11 Group.

There was no doubt that there was a definite degree of animosity towards the Big Wing from among 11 Group. For the higher command of 11 Group the issue was often that the Wing did not always appear when it was needed. There were also problems with respect to R/T ranges and frequencies. 11 Group controllers were not able to talk to

12 Group aircraft and vice versa when 12 Group aircraft crossed into 11 Group airspace. Confusion was also caused to Observer Corps and A A Gun Defences who could not be informed of their movements.

By mid August Park was complaining about the chaos that was being caused by the free-ranging interventions by the 12 Group squadrons out of Duxford. In a letter of 27th August he commended the support that he had received from 10 Group and their consistent help in covering the Portsmouth area. In the same letter he stated that 12 Group had not shown the same desire to co-operate by dispatching their squadrons to the places requested.

There had been occasions when both Debden and North Weald had been heavily bombed, when they were supposed to have been covered by 12 Group squadrons. Park suspected that they had simply gone elsewhere to find a fight, which was probably not too far from the truth. On one occasion when the Duxford Wing turned up over Dover, the Observer Corps mistakenly took it for another enemy raid that was being mounted.

Leigh-Mallory ignored Park's complaints and Dowding, who should probably have interceded, was too preoccupied to give the developing problem the attention that it deserved. The pendulum had definitely begun to swing against Park.

Douglas was obviously highly instrumental in this, but it is most unlikely that this was uppermost in his mind. Douglas was simply keen on shooting down Germans and he was convinced that using the Big Wing was the best way to do it. He was keen that the Big Wing should be universally regarded as the way forward and the fact that his ideas were being used as a political tool in the power struggle between two rival AOCs was of no particular concern to him.

He later expressed his admiration for Keith Park, calling him a 'splendid fellow' and implying that the only reason that Park failed to appreciate the efficacy of the Big Wing was that he had been so bowed down by fatigue caused by the weight of his responsibilities.

He also later maintained that he had always regarded the Big Wing principle as being far more suitable for 12 Group squadrons than for those of 11 Group. He reiterated that he regarded it as being complementary rather than an alternative to 11 Group strategy.

In the aftermath of the Battle of Britain on 17th October a high level conference was called at the Air Ministry to discuss fighter formation tactics. The agenda seemed to assume that it would be agreed that wing formations were ipso facto a good thing and that the real issue was how best to use them.

The members of the conference included an Air Chief Marshal, two Air Marshals, four Air Vice-Marshals, three Air Commodores, a Group Captain, a Wing Commander, plus the official minute taker. There was some surprise when Leigh-Mallory arrived accompanied by Acting Squadron Leader Douglas Bader.

Discussion has raged as to whether or not it was right for Leigh-Mallory to have taken Douglas to the meeting. To Douglas it was an opportunity to get his theories made known directly to the Air Council, while to the ever ambitious Leigh-Mallory it was an opportunity to provide ammunition that would eclipse his rival.

According to the official minutes, Douglas's input to the conference was significant, but not extensive. The official record of his total contribution amounted to just 41 words: "Squadron Leader Bader said that from his practical experience time was the essence of the problem; if enough warning could be given to bring a large number of fighters into position there was no doubt they could get most effective results".

When it was Leigh-Mallory's turn to speak he was eloquent in his criticism of his colleague and his strategy. He boasted that he could get five Duxford squadrons into the air within six minutes and within 25 minutes they could be over Hornchurch. In practice this was a little optimistic because on one occasion it had taken all of 17 minutes for the Wing to get airborne and another 20 minutes for them to set course from base.

It was clear that there was no support for Hugh Dowding from those present and consequently very little for Keith Park. Dowding had spent four years preparing Fighter Command for a battle that had just been comprehensively won, but by October 1940 he was exhausted and not prepared to fight another battle.

One thing that Douglas didn't know at the time was the part that had been played by Peter Macdonald, his adjutant at 242 Squadron. For good number of years Peter Macdonald had been the Conservative MP for the Isle of Wight and as such had a considerable amount of political influence. He had been impressed by Douglas's theories, having heard him expound on them to numerous people on numerous occasions. He managed to arrange a meeting with Winston Churchill.

The upshot of this seems to have been that Churchill prodded Sir Archibald Sinclair, the Secretary of State for Air, to make a fact-finding visit to Duxford. Sinclair came away from his visit "feeling that there was a conflict of operational views between 11 Group and 12 Group". Douglas had obviously been far from reluctant to express his opinion that 11 Group were not making the best use of the Big Wing.

Sinclair then asked Harold Balfour, the Under Secretary of State to make a confirmatory visit and to record his findings. Balfour concluded in his report that matters had reached crisis point, with pilots in the Wing feeling "resentful against 11 Group and its AOC because they were being denied opportunities of shooting down Germans simply because on every occasion when the wing had gone up it had arrived too late".

Dowding was very much aware of the fact that it was Douglas's theories that had been the cause of what he considered to be unfair criticism of 11 Group. This effectively was gross insubordination on Douglas's part that could easily have led to disciplinary action.

While Dowding acknowledged Douglas's undoubted bravery and would not countenance any action against him, he felt that he suffered from "over-development of the critical faculty" and that consequently he

A Dornier Do17 burns on the ground "somewhere in England". The Do17 was designed to be a fast, low level strike bomber and proved its worth in the early years of the war before being phased out in 1942.

should be posted to a station where he would be "kept in better control". He should be made to understand that he was a mere squadron leader and not the architect of Fighter Command strategy.

Dowding also made it quite clear that he felt the Big Wing to be a waste of precious resources and that it should be disbanded.

In the climate of the time this was nothing short of heresy on Dowding's part. By now it was Leigh-Mallory who had the major influence at the Air Ministry and he was advocating expanding the Big Wing from five to six squadrons.

As a result Dowding's views were ignored and on 13th November Sir Archibald Sinclair informed him that he was to be relieved of his post as C-in-C Fighter Command in order to head a supply acquisition mission in America; his place as C-in-C Fighter Command would be taken by Sholto Douglas.

Keith Park was also utterly drained and within a month he too was relieved of his command. He saw this as a great insult and never really got over his bitterness. He regarded it as the final twist of the knife when he learnt that his replacement as C-in-C of 11 Group was none other than

Leigh-Mallory. When he was offered a post on the Air Staff he turned it down because by then he regarded the Air Ministry as a place of intrigue, so he took over Group Training Command.

Many felt that both men had been very shabbily treated and the controversy surrounding their redeployment has never really been resolved. Meanwhile Douglas stayed at Duxford in command of 242 Squadron.

He continued to have a deep regard and respect for both Dowding and Park. He was very upset when Dowding was not made a Marshal of the Royal Air Force when he retired and in later years he never missed a chance to lobby any important figures who might have influence to remedy this.

1968 saw the making of the film The Battle of Britain. The film far exceeded its massive $12 million budget and went on to make a worldwide loss of $10 million. The former RAF Duxford was used for many of the exteriors and Douglas, along with a number of his Battle of Britain contemporaries, spent a day there to watch the filming. Among their number was Hugh Dowding, now old and frail and confined to a wheel chair, but it was Douglas who insisted on spending the day pushing him around the airfield.

As for Keith Park, after two years at Group Training Command, rested and invigorated he took over the defence of Malta and subsequently filled a number of other high power jobs before eventually retiring and returning to his native New Zealand.

After Douglas left the RAF and returned to work for Shell, he always made a point of trying to call on Keith Park whenever he visited Australia or New Zealand. Their respect for each other was mutual, although neither ever raised with the other the tactical controversies of 1940.

When Keith Park died in 1974 at the age of eighty-two, a memorial service was held for him at the RAF church of St Clement Danes in London and Douglas was asked to give the address. He summed up his feelings in the following way: "They were busy times, exhilarating times, with never a thought that we might lose the battle, Keith Park was one of us. We all shared the great experience."

Wing Leader

Shortly after he took over as C-in-C of Fighter Command, Sholto Douglas called together a select group of officers, including Douglas Bader of 242 Squadron, Bob Tuck of 257 Squadron and Adolph 'Sailor' Malan of 74 Squadron to discuss future armament for fighters that were due to come on stream the following year.

Up until then the usual armament for Hurricanes and Spitfires had been eight .303 calibre Browning machine guns, but there was concern at the growing trend of the Luftwaffe to increasingly fit more armour to its bombers. This additional protection meant that they were getting harder to shoot down with the relatively small calibre machine-guns of the RAF's standard armament.

The C-in-C wanted to know his squadron commanders' opinions as to whether or not RAF fighters should be fitted with cannons in order to provide greater hitting power. Douglas immediately leapt in to say that there was no doubt in his mind that they should stick with the eight Brownings since they were tried and tested and familiar to everyone. Tuck and Malan disagreed and expressed strong views that the explosive and armour-piercing shells of the cannons would increase the chance of bringing down more of the enemy.

Douglas, however, had been familiar with the serious problems that 19 Squadron had experienced at Duxford when it had acquired new Spitfires that were fitted with experimental cannons. These had kept jamming, often with serious results and it was only after Hugh Dowding's personal intervention that these aircraft had been replaced. As a result Douglas was firmly against cannons and was never one to accept any view other than

A squadron of Spitfires lined up on the ground. During the Battle of Britain this would have been a rare sight as aircraft grouped together like this would have been vulnerable to Luftwaffe attacks.

his own. His reaction was typically forceful: "Bobbie, for God's sake, don't talk rot! You too Sailor - the pair of you think this is a bloody miracle weapon."

At that point a furious row broke out and it was only after the C-in C's calm intervention that the meeting quietened down.

Eventually it was decided that when the new Spitfire VB was introduced in the summer of 1941, the standard equipment for it would be two 20-mm cannon with four .303-inch machine guns. Douglas, however, refused to accept a cannon-armed machine and for a while continued to fly a Spitfire II until he acquired a comparatively rare Spitfire VA that was armed solely with machine guns.

Although he had long since retired, Lord Trenchard was still highly regarded as the founding father of the Royal Air Force and continued to have a great deal of influence at the Air Ministry. During the autumn of 1940 he paid a visit to Charles 'Peter' Portal, Chief of Air Staff, to argue the view that the time had now come for the RAF to take on a more offensive role and engage in sweeps over enemy territory.

Circumstances had dictated that during the Battle of Britain a purely defensive strategy was required by Fighter Command, but now there was a general feeling that the time had come to break free from this defensive outlook and to return to a more aggressive mentality that had been so much a feature of the operations of the Royal Flying Corps over the Western Front during the Great War.

Sholto Douglas met with his group commanders at the end of November to further stress this "need to get away from the purely defensive outlook". A week or two after this, Park was relieved of his post at Uxbridge and Leigh-Mallory took over as AOC 11 Group.

Following the 17th October conference, in spite of Hugh Dowding's wish to see otherwise, Douglas had continued to lead 242 Squadron from Duxford. One of Leigh-Mallory's first moves after taking over as AOC 11 Group, was to arrange for 242 Squadron and Douglas to be moved from RAF Duxford to RAF Martlesham Heath, one of his own 11 Group stations.

Big Wing operations were definitely becoming the order of the day. Leigh-Mallory was now arguing for a super wing, made up of three wings, each of three squadrons that together would produce a formidable formation of 108 aircraft. There was still some scepticism about the big wing principle, but the important factor was the 100% support from Sholto Douglas, the new C-in-C of Fighter Command and that was all that mattered.

This, of course, was music to the ears of Douglas. In his view it was entirely right and proper to use force and numerical superiority to take the war to the enemy. This was the whole essence of his Big Wing concept.

One of Leigh-Mallory's innovations was the introduction of what became known as 'Rhubarbs' and 'Circuses', both of which took place over enemy territory. Rhubarbs were when a single fighter or a pair of fighters would use cloud cover to mask their movements as they flew over to harass the enemy on the ground. A Circus was when a larger fighter force would be used in better weather, sometimes accompanying a limited number of bombers, to make the enemy come up and fight and force them onto the defensive.

Douglas was allowed to stage a Rhubarb sortie early in the second week of January 1941 and Leigh-Mallory gave him a prominent place in the very first Circus raid on France the following day.

Douglas found it very frustrating when the expected enemy did not materialise and he resorted to aerobatics to work off his energy. On the second Circus operation in which 242 were supposed to take part, the engine of Douglas's Hurricane refused to start. He caused some raised eyebrows by deciding that if he was unable to go, none of the rest of his squadron would go either.

By now Douglas was achieving celebrity status. His fame had spread to the United States where he was being promoted in the media as one of the RAF's top ten aces, but in Britain he was even more famous. He regularly featured in newspapers and magazines and in February 1941 he was chosen to make a BBC radio broadcast about his first combat with 242 Squadron.

He was definitely being groomed for higher things and confirmation of this came in mid-March 1941. Earlier in the month Leigh-Mallory had sent for him to tell him that Sholto Douglas had decided the each sector station should have a wing commander flying and he offered Douglas first choice of Tangmere or Biggin Hill.

Douglas chose Tangmere because he considered that since Biggin Hill was only 50 minutes drive from London, there would be a great temptation for his pilots to want to rush off to the Savoy after a hard day's fighting and then have to fight again the following morning. Douglas felt that Tangmere, located 3 miles east of Chichester, was just that bit safer.

The Biggin Hill Wing was offered to the South African ace Sailor Malan. Adolph (Sailor) Malan had spent a number of years as a merchant navy officer with the Union Castle Line. His many visits to Hamburg and his conversations with port officials and other Germans that he met had convinced him that war was inevitable and in 1935 he settled in Britain and joined the RAF.

Having completed his training he was posted to 74 Squadron in December 1936 and somewhat unusually stayed with 74, rising to the rank of squadron leader before taking over as wing leader at Biggin Hill in 1941. Douglas and Sailor were firm friends, but they were also great rivals.

There were five Spitfire Wings in all, the other three being at Kenley, North Weald and Hornchurch. Each had three squadrons and each was led by a Wing Commander.

The pros and cons of the use of Big Wings still rumbled on. When in January 1941 Leigh-Mallory conducted a paper exercise to see what difference a Big Wing would have made to the outcome of the Battle of Britain, the advocates refused to be put off even when the unfortunate result was a resounding victory for the Luftwaffe.

Adolph "Sailor" Malan was a South African pilot who shot down 27 German aircraft, formulated a set of combat rules and inspired adulation among his fellow pilots.

This paper exercise was considered to be of no consequence. Wing enthusiasts continued to maintain that big formations were very appropriate for the kind of offensive action that was now being contemplated. Any opposition was considered to be out of the question.

Sceptics, whose squadrons had lost substantial numbers of pilots during initial attempts to organise cross-channel operations and who expressed reluctance at "offering themselves up as sacrificial lambs to the whims of unsound tacticians", were promptly posted away and their units broken up.

Douglas's new Wing had three Spitfire squadrons, 145, 610 and 616. Within half an hour of arriving at Tangmere he had commandeered an aircraft, "to get the feel again" and within two hours he had two of the squadrons in the air together for a snoop for enemy aircraft.

Eventually the operations room at Tangmere called him up to say that there were no enemy aircraft about and that he was to return to base. Douglas's typical reaction was: "Okay, just one more minute. You never know."

Douglas continued to be mad keen on aerobatics, maintaining that no man could master his aircraft unless he could control it in all attitudes. His lack of legs actually gave him something of an advantage because in tight turns, where a pilot would often black out when the blood rushed from his head to his legs, in Douglas's case this obviously did not happen. His frequent, almost daily displays were, as Johnnie Johnson of 616 Squadron later recalled, "the delight of the ground crews and we all strolled out on to the tarmac to watch the wing commander".

A few months after Douglas arrived at Tangmere, a certain Flight Lieutenant E P Gibbs was posted to 616 Squadron. 'Gibbo' was also particularly skilled at aerobatics and one day Douglas and Johnnie Johnson were standing together watching Gibbs doing a fine display of aerobatics when it became clear that he was about to attempt three upward rolls. Johnson knew that Douglas had only ever managed two.

"He'll never do it old boy," said Douglas, but when Gibbs completed a third upward roll with apparent ease, Johnson thought that Douglas 'was bloody livid'. There were no more aerobatic displays after that for quite some time.

As soon as he had arrived at Tangmere Douglas had set to work redeploying his leaders. Those that he didn't like were posted away and he brought in many of his favourites from 242 Squadron. This obviously denuded 242 of its most experienced pilots and it also caused some disruption at Tangmere, where pilots who had got used to working as a team now found themselves working with new leaders.

Douglas also managed to arrange for his favourite controller, Woody Woodhall to be transferred to Tangmere. This all made pretty good sense because as a new wing leader Douglas needed to have subordinate leaders and a controller that he knew he could work with.

He still managed to get away with short-circuiting official procedures. When he wanted his Spitfire IIs of 616 Squadron to be retrofitted with metal ailerons to improve roll and turn, his simply flew the squadron to the Southampton factory and demanded that they be fitted on the spot.

Now that he was of senior enough rank to make tactical decisions, he began to talk through, test and adopt major changes in basic formation tactics. The standard fighter formation at the beginning of the war had been a tight 'vic' of three aircraft. This proved to be highly dangerous in a combat situation since pilots had to spend so much time concentrating on maintaining formation without crashing into each other that they were unable to keep searching the sky for attacking enemy fighters.

These changes of formation and tactics were very much a matter of trial and error and since Douglas was always incredibly keen about new ideas that seemed to be good, he would insist on having his way with them. It was generally accepted that in the event of the idea not meeting up to expectations, Douglas would immediately switch to the opposite view, with even greater enthusiasm.

As a result of his period of trial and error Douglas began to use the 'finger four' formation, which coincidentally was the formation that was used by the Luftwaffe after it had been developed by German pilots fighting with the Condor Legion during the Spanish Civil War.

Actually a number of other leading commanders, such as Bob Tuck had also taken to flying in pairs rather than in threes, so this change in tactics was not Douglas's sole preserve. The difference was that by then Douglas had a higher profile than most, so it is perhaps understandable that his name became linked with the new tactical formations.

Douglas was now a dominant figure in the flying hierarchy of Fighter Command. Of the three squadrons in his wing he preferred to fly with 616, commanded by Cranwell graduate Billy Burton. Although younger than Douglas, the two hit it off straight away and Burton was quite happy for Douglas to lead.

He flew the Wing in loose sections of four aircraft, with two pairs flying together. On Douglas's left, his number two was the dependable Alan Smith from South Shields, while the other pair on Douglas's right was led by Hugh Dundas, otherwise known as 'Cocky', with Johnnie Johnson as his number two.

Douglas's amazing qualities of leadership enabled him to bring the best out of the men who served with him. The four made an excellent team and within a couple of years both Dundas and Johnson were to become two of the RAF's most successful wing leaders and Alan Smith was to go from sergeant to flight commander. Dundas's assessment of Douglas was quite simple: "He was bloody marvellous, that's all there was to it."

The Rhubarbs and Circuses continued, but they were not achieving the success that had been hoped for. Luftwaffe fighters had simply refused to engage. Their strategy was to lurk behind and pick off strays and stragglers, or to wait until they knew that the RAF formations were low on fuel before making quick darting passes.

The RAF pilots had the supreme disadvantage that if they were shot down over enemy territory, if they survived they would almost certainly be taken prisoner. By the second week of March the Wing had lost 17 pilots against the optimistic claim of 13 enemy aircraft shot down.

In spite of the losses, the Chief of Air Staff, Charles Portal and Leigh-Mallory, C-in-C of Fighter Command insisted on continuing with the policy. At a high level conference Arthur Harris, C-in-C of Bomber Command, expressed the view that surely in order for attacks to be profitable, we either had to shoot down more fighters than we lost or we had to inflict material damage on the enemy and it seemed that neither was happening.

Charles Portal took great exception to this line of thinking, saying that he believed that the operations improved morale and that he would willingly accept even heavier losses if it threw the enemy on the defensive and gave our units moral superiority by doing most of the fighting on the other side.

Sholto Douglas expressed a view that if 'damaged' claims were factored in with the 'destroyed' claims then the ratio of losses favoured the RAF. There was obviously no going back.

Leigh-Mallory was effectively given the green light and in the middle of April 1941 he called together his sector station commanders and wing leaders to a meeting at Uxbridge. He told them that the RAF was about to go on the offensive and that it would do wonders for pilot morale.

Sailor Malan, not normally noted for his outspokenness, interrupted the AOC to tell him that he was trying to do the impossible. His comments were simply swept aside by Leigh-Mallory who put Malan's outburst down to fatigue and told him to take a rest.

On the other hand Douglas of course was raring to go.

Rhubarbs and
Circuses

In fact the weather that year was so bad that it was June before conditions had improved sufficiently for the Tangmere Wing to begin the new offensive and to operate en masse. Once again the enemy fighters kept out of the way of these large formations and as before they were content to just pick off the occasional stray. Limited fuel capacity meant that the RAF fighters could not fly very far inland and consequently were unlikely to inflict much damage.

Douglas was frustrated by the lack of action and was furious when other Wings, such as Sailor Malan's Biggin Hill Wing, managed to score successes while the Tangmere Wing ended up with nothing. This all changed somewhat after 22nd June following the German invasion of the Soviet Union, codenamed Operation Barbarossa.

New tactics raised the level of RAF aggression and in addition to the major goal of destroying as many enemy aircraft as possible, it was also hoped that this increased aggression by the RAF would not only limit the number of enemy aircraft being transferred to Russia, but would actually encourage the Luftwaffe to withdraw fighters from Russia to meet the increasing attacks in the West.

Circus operations became more complex and the Wings were in the thick of things from late June right through July. The fighter Wings flew in close-escort with small formations of bombers, giving close-support and providing top cover. The aim was to draw up enemy aircraft before the main force of the escort wing started to run short of fuel and had to turn for home. If all went according to plan, the target-withdrawal wing would arrive to engage the enemy just as the fighters of the escort wing were beginning to leave.

A squadron of Spitfires takes off to carry out a "rhubarb" in the late summer of 1941.

If the weather was favourable, there would generally be two or three sweeps almost every day. On days when the weather was bad, Douglas was in the habit of mounting unauthorised Rhubarb flights. Ostensibly he and his section would be engaging in 'local flying' but in reality he would lead them across the Channel in search of trouble.

Douglas always flew with 616 Squadron and was said to have been utterly fearless. He was always the last to leave a scene of action, hanging on in case there was something to shoot at.

Another example of Douglas's total disregard of danger stood out in the minds of the pilots who flew with him. This was his habit of taking out his pipe and cheerfully lighting up while on the way back from a mission. He would seemingly be completely oblivious to the tank of high octane petrol that was located just behind his head and the likelihood of an imminent explosion if it had been damaged in any way. He would sit there at the controls contentedly puffing away and grinning at the way the other members of his section discreetly drifted away to put a safer distance between themselves and him.

By the end of the first week in August, some seven weeks since the launch of Operation Barbarossa, the Tangmere Wing had claimed over

25 definite kills. Douglas himself had added six more kills to his personal score and had been awarded a bar to his existing DSO for "his high qualities of leadership and courage that have been an inspiration to us all."

Although he was generally described as being a friendly type, Douglas was also said to be a grim and dedicated killer of Germans. He also had vast reserves of pent-up energy and the impromptu sorties where he led his section across the Channel in poor weather were his way of enjoying himself and letting off steam.

Although Douglas revelled in this sort of thing, most of the other pilots hated it. Flying in pairs under a low cloud base not only risked the danger of being bounced from above, but there was also the real danger of being hit by flak. Spitfires and Hurricanes both had liquid cooled engines and in both types the coolant tanks located beneath the nose were a particular vulnerability. If this tank should be punctured, the coolant would rapidly drain away and the engine would seize up.

By the middle of June eight RAF pilots had been lost on these Rhubarb missions for no appreciable gain. Many pilots regarded them as "acts of sheer madness or a dirty date with fate." Johnnie Johnson later confessed that he loathed Rhubarbs "with a deep, dark, hatred".

Circuses were also fraught with danger and Douglas always insisted in leading from the air, rather than relying on the controller back at base. It was no simple matter to direct 36 Spitfires that could well be operating with other fighter wings or bomber formations. Rendezvousing with other formations brought the serious risk of collisions.

There were other problems. Since he always insisted on leading every wing operation at the head of 616 Squadron, the other two squadrons in the Wing felt ignored. Meanwhile the CO of 616 Squadron never got a chance to lead his own men.

Novice pilots complained that Douglas was very brusque and did not have much time for anyone who was not an ace. Sergeant pilots often felt that he was not very keen on them and rumours circulated that he wanted to create an officers-only wing.

His insistence on leading every wing sortie meant that nobody else ever got the experience of wing leadership. Sailor Malan's approach at Biggin Hill was rather different. While he always led the first mission of the day, he preferred to hand over to one of the other pilots for further missions while he stayed back at base to catch up on the paperwork.

Since Douglas was such a 'hands on' leader, the sheer pressure began to take its toll. At one point over a period of seven days he led ten sweeps and he was fast reaching the point where there was a danger that sheer fatigue would begin to impair his judgement.

James "Johnnie" Johnson, one of Bader's most devoted followers, climbs out of his fighter while being filmed by a news crew at RAF Kings Cliffe in the summer of 1941. The exploits of Fighter Command made them popular subjects for the media.

He was inclined to bully his ground crews, one of whom described him as "the most pompous chap I ever met". Another said how "he was aggressive nearly all the time, never a 'please' or 'thank you'". The ground crews found this to be in marked contrast to other pilots who appreciated the importance of maintaining a good relationship with the men who looked after their aircraft.

Extravagant claims were being made of the numbers of enemy aircraft that were being shot down by the Wing on these operations and these figures were used to justify their continuance. In reality the victory claims were usually inflated by a factor of about 5:1, so the picture was not nearly so rosy as the optimists maintained.

This rosy picture masked the seriousness of the RAF casualty rates. These continued to mount to the point where the RAF was actually losing three aircraft for every one that was lost by the Luftwaffe.

Between 21st June and 4th July 40 RAF pilots were lost and this was during a period when Fighter Command operations were considered to have been particularly successful. In just over seven weeks, between 20th June and 10th August, 616 Squadron alone lost 12 pilots.

But as far as Douglas was concerned everything continued to run like clockwork and he refused to accept any argument to the contrary. If anyone voiced an opinion that suggested otherwise, he was simply told that he was being windy and that was the end of it.

Leigh-Mallory held regular conferences two or three times a week to discuss the state of things. The pattern for these was that after the last mission of the day, Douglas, Woody and one of the squadron commanders from Tangmere would fly up to Northolt, where they would be met by a car that would take them the 11 Group HQ in Uxbridge. Here they would join the other Sector Commanders, Wing Leaders and Squadron Commanders.

At one of these conferences, when one of the wing leaders questioned whether the benefits of these operations over France were really outweighing the costs, Douglas immediately jumped in with: "Hell, old boy, you can't just spend the rest of your life doing slow rolls over the aerodrome". Douglas's influence was such that while there could be arguments over tactics, his opinions usually dominated and as a result there was never any serious questioning of the offensive as such.

By now Douglas had reached the dizzy heights of being regarded as a priceless national asset and there was discussion as to the advisability of allowing him to continue operational flying, but Douglas would hear none of this. All he wanted to do was to shoot down more enemy aircraft and improve his personal score. Although he insisted that his pilots took regular breaks from operations, he never took a break himself and insisted on leading every mission, sometimes two and often three times a day, right through the summer.

As was to be expected, fatigue began to catch up with him, although he refused to recognise or accept this. Like other wing and squadron commanders Douglas had been on operations more or less continuously for eighteen months. He was literarily driving himself into the ground. Both Peter Macdonald, who was now at Tangmere, and Woody urged him to take a rest, but Douglas would not listen.

Meanwhile at Biggin Hill, Sailor Malan was also feeling the strain. He too initially resisted suggestions that he should take a break, but he came to realise that sheer fatigue was beginning to impair his skills. In late July, in an act of great courage, he told the AOC straight out that he felt that he should be relieved.

Leigh-Mallory recognised what was happening and immediately granted Sailor's request and then flew down to Tangmere with the intention of ordering Douglas to do likewise. He told Douglas that all the other wing leaders had all been taken off operations, but again Douglas would have none of it.

He wanted to 'see the season out' as he put it and increase his personal score from its current official total of 20½ kills. Leigh-Mallory was not inclined to cross one of his star fighter pilots, so he backed down and let Douglas have his own way.

This did not please everyone at Tangmere where there was a certain amount of concern, certainly among the rank and file that the wing commander was not as sharp as he had previously been. It seems that as August moved into its second week there were those in the Tangmere Wing who were in a near-mutinous state by what they regarded as Douglas's reckless leadership as he strove to increase his personal score.

Brian Lane (centre) flew with Bader in the early days of the war and during the Battle of Britain commanded No.19 Squadron and frequently co-operated with Bader when he commanded No.242 Squadron.

The concern at Douglas's insistence to continue operational flying spread outside the RAF where there were murmurings that Douglas was effectively riding for a fall. The Daily Mirror's influential 'Cassandra' more or less predicted this when in July he wrote in his column: "I propose that Douglas Bader be prohibited from ever stepping into an aircraft again. Such men as he are too valuable to England!"

This relentless pressure obviously could not go on for ever and the end finally came on Saturday 9th August.

Shot Down

Things had not gone right from the word go. To begin with Douglas's usual wingman, Alan Smith, had been grounded with a heavy head cold. Quite naturally there were strict rules about pilots flying with blocked sinuses in unpressurised aircraft, so he had to stay behind. His replacement was Jeff West and although Jeff was far from being a novice, he was not used to working so closely with Douglas.

Secondly, one of the three squadrons missed its rendezvous with the other two. The three squadrons of the Tangmere Wing were actually based at different airfields although they were all very close to each other. Only 610 Squadron was actually based at Tangmere, while Douglas's favourite, 616 Squadron, was based at RAF Westhampnett on the Duke of Richmond's Goodwood Estate and Stan Turner's 145 Squadron was based at RAF Merston. Westhampnett and Merston were really satellite stations of Tangmere..

To Stan Turner's great annoyance it had recently been decided that 145 Squadron was to be rested and they had been posted up to Yorkshire. Their place at RAF Merston had been taken by 41 Squadron under the command of Canadian Elmer Gaunce. At the beginning of August 41 Squadron was still finding its feet and it uncharacteristically failed to meet up with the other two squadrons.

This is when things began to go seriously wrong as the mission continued with only two squadrons, 616 and 610, rather than three. The next problem came when Douglas discovered that his Spitfire's airspeed indicator was not working. This was particularly serious because without an ASI there was no way of judging speeds and timings since you don't know how fast you are going. Cocky Dundas took over the lead for this part of the mission.

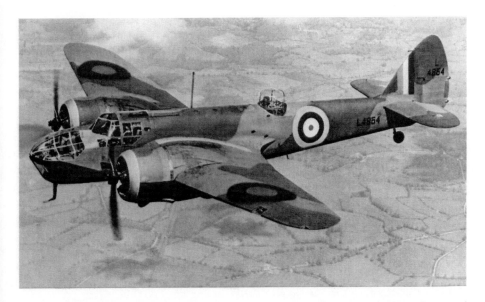

A Bristol Blenheim light bomber. It was one of these aircraft that dropped Bader's spare leg to him after he had been shot down and captured by the Germans.

A further problem then arose when Douglas discovered that his RT set wasn't functioning properly. One of Douglas's numerous golden rules for pilots was that given the circumstances and the number of things stacked against him, at this point he should have returned home, but as Laddie Lucas later said: "Douglas was not that sort of chap."

A message then came through from Woody, the controller at Tangmere, warning of large numbers of enemy aircraft in their vicinity. Almost immediately various pilots began calling in to report sightings of Bf 109s behind, above and below them, but Douglas's attention became focused on a dozen 109s that were ahead of 616 Squadron and about two or three thousand feet below. He regarded this as a classic attack position and immediately led his section of four Spitfires into the fray.

Cocky Dundas was one of the four and he immediately suspected a trap and this is exactly what it was. Enemy fighters suddenly swooped down from above and behind and in no time the hunters had become the hunted. With no functioning airspeed indicator Douglas had not been able to judge his speed and he flashed through the enemy so fast that he lost the rest of his section and when he pulled up, the sky seemed empty.

He was now in a very dangerous position, being a lone aircraft in an empty sky and potentially a sitting duck. Another of his golden rules was that if a pilot ever found himself in this position, alone in the sky, he should drop down and head for home immediately, but like most of

Hugh "Cocky" Dundas was flying alongside Bader on the final mission on 9 August 1941. The two men got separated in the combat which saw Bader go down.

his golden rules, while Douglas was quite insistent that they should be obeyed by other pilots he did not consider that they should apply to him.

He looked around and saw a formation of three pairs of Bf 109s flying ahead of him. He sized up the situation and decided that he had an excellent chance of picking off a couple of the enemy before the others had a chance to react.

He came up behind and did manage to pick off the rear one. He was about to go for the leader when the others spotted him. He then made what he called his final mistake. Yet another of his golden rules was always turn towards the enemy, but he turned the other way. His aircraft gave an almighty shudder and when he looked behind he saw that the entire tail section of his aircraft had disappeared.

He suddenly found himself in the position of having to abandon his aircraft over the St Omer region. Fortunately he had been flying at about 24,000 feet, because he had some difficulty in getting out of his stricken aircraft when one of his metal legs was trapped.

The aircraft was plummeting earthwards, with bits breaking off all the time and still Douglas couldn't get free. Eventually he pulled the rip-cord of his parachute and as it opened he was pulled from the cockpit and leather strap that held his leg promptly broke. By now he was down to about 6,000 feet.

Fortunately there was no problem with his parachute and as he gently floated towards the ground he heard the sound of a 109 pass very close by him. He must have presented a strange-looking picture to the startled farm workers as they looked up to see this peculiar figure drifting towards them with what appeared to be one good leg and an empty trouser leg flapping in the breeze.

Within minutes of landing the Germans had picked him up. They could hardly believe their good fortune since Douglas was almost as famous to the Luftwaffe as he was to the RAF. He was taken to hospital in St Omer suffering from concussion but apart from that he was comparatively unscathed.

Douglas's Spitfire continued to disintegrate as it fell to the ground and no wreckage has ever been discovered. His damaged leg was found in a

The main square of St Omer, where Bader was taken for treatment after he was captured by the Germans. His concussion proved to be only temporary.

field and a German technician patched it up and it was returned to him at the hospital in St Omer.

To Göring's later fury, Douglas was invited to the officers' mess at Audembert, home of Adolph Galland's Wing, Jagdgeschwader 26, or fighter wing 26. JG 26 had nine squadrons, or staffels that were deployed at several airfields in the Pas de Calais area.

Douglas immediately thought that this was a golden opportunity to steal a plane and escape, but although his captors let him sit in the cockpit of a Bf 109, a German pilot stood on each of its wings, holding a drawn and cocked pistol just to make sure that the aircraft stayed firmly on the ground.

At Audembert it was initially suggested to Douglas that he had been shot down by an NCO pilot. Douglas was reported to have found this as being "an intolerable idea", so the tactful Germans produced a handsome young flying officer who was then introduced to him as his 'victorious opponent'. However, Douglas was convinced that he had been brought down as a result of a collision.

There is a strange twist to this story that occurred 40 years later in Australia. Douglas had gone to Sydney to open an air show and among the many people who were introduced to him during the day was a former Luftwaffe pilot by the name of Max Meyer. Max Meyer had been living in Australia for a number of years and as Laddie Lucas put it, the two "exchanged customary pleasantries but no more".

The following day Douglas was somewhat startled when all the Australian newspapers were full of an interview that Meyer had given to an Australian journalist in which he had said that he was the pilot who had been responsible for shooting down Douglas Bader on 9th August 1941. Strangely at no time was this mentioned when the two men had met the previous day.

The story provoked further investigation of Luftwaffe records back in England. It was discovered that there was indeed an entry for 9th August 1941. It appeared that between 11.25 and 11.30 a 109 pilot by the name of

Oberfeldwebel Meyer, a flight sergeant in RAF terms, serving with No 6 Staffel of Galland's Wing, had shot down a Spitfire over St Omer.

The timing was certainly right and in his report Meyer stated that he had followed his victim down, which certainly tied in with Douglas's account of a 109 passing close by him during his descent.

Of course the first question that arises is that if this was indeed the true story, why was there a delay of 40 years before telling it?

Perhaps more important is that if this really was true, how was it that the mighty Nazi propaganda machine did not make the most of a story of how the most famous wing commander in the RAF had been shot down by a lowly sergeant pilot?

Douglas of course rejected the story out of hand.

"My dear boy, if a sergeant pilot had shot me down, they would have had him goose-stepping down the Unter den Linden."

The true cause of Douglas's crash has never satisfactorily been resolved. To his dying day he maintained his belief that in turning away from the enemy his Spitfire's tail assembly had been ripped off when he collided with a 109. However, the same sort of damage was known to have been the result of a good burst of 109 canon fire and when he appeared on Desert Island Discs in November 1981, he did admit to Roy Plomley the possibility that he might actually have been shot down.

There are basically three possible causes of his crash. It is generally accepted that he was either in collision with a 109 or was shot down by one. The third possibility is somewhat more intriguing. There is evidence to support the view that Douglas was actually shot down by another Spitfire.

616 Squadron lost another pilot on 9th August, Flight Lieutenant 'Buck' Casson who was taken prisoner after being forced to crash land his damaged Spitfire into a field. Following their release at the end of the war, Casson wrote to Douglas giving his account of what had happened earlier in the day. He said the following: "When we dived to attack those Me109s

that were climbing up in formation I was to starboard and behind you with three other aircraft of B Flight ... I watched you attack those Me 109s that were climbing up in formation. I was well throttled back in the dive as the other three started to fall behind and I wanted to keep the flight together. I attacked from the rear and after having a squirt at two 109s flying together I left them for a single one flying alone. I finished nearly all my cannon ammo up on this boy who finally baled out at 6000 ft having lost most of his tail unit ..."

Casson made his initial attack at 24,000 feet and the pilot bailed out at 6,000 feet. Douglas had been hit when he was flying at approximately 24,000 feet and struggled for some time before he was able to get out of his cockpit.

From the rear a 109 and a Spitfire look remarkably similar. Is it possible that the single 109 that was identified by Buck Casson was actually Douglas's Spitfire?. That being the case, could Douglas have been shot down by Buck Casson?

The letter was heavily edited and only sections are in the public domain. There is the intriguing speculation that Douglas knew all along that it was Buck Casson who had shot him down and that he later endeavoured to shield Buck by fabricating a story about being in collision with a 109.

These are fascinating questions and although it would be interesting to know what really happened, the fact must be faced that the event took place over 70 years ago so probably we will never know the true answer.

One thing is certain and that is that Douglas was largely responsible for his own downfall:

* for a start he refused to go off operations when it was suggested to him that he was exhausted and that the time had come for him to take a break;

* secondly, with a faulty radio and a u/s airspeed indicator he should have turned back rather than insisting on continuing to lead the wing;

* thirdly after becoming isolated, he should have headed for home rather than hanging about looking for trouble;

* finally he broke another of his own golden rules by turning away from the enemy rather than meeting it head on.

To some it had been a foregone conclusion that since no man was invincible, Douglas's luck could not last for ever. Indeed it had been less than a fortnight since Cassandra had predicted as such.

Douglas's supreme self-confidence in his ability had worn off on everyone else, with the result that nobody, least of all himself, thought that anything bad would ever happen to him. He had in fact taken on the mantle of invincibility.

It is easy to understand the shock, horror and downright disbelief at the news of his downfall. Woody was among the first to suspect that something was wrong when the airwaves went ominously quiet. When Douglas was in the air he normally kept up an almost constant chatter, generally interspersed with what could be termed as extremely 'fruity language', but suddenly there was nothing - a sure sign that all was not what it ought to be.

Woody tried calling 'Dogsbody', Douglas's call sign and after a pause Johnnie Johnson replied that they had been heavily engaged and that he had last seen Dogsbody diving on a 109 and they hadn't seen him since.

When they returned to base the pilots reported that several enemy aircraft had been shot down and that in addition to Douglas, Buck Casson had also failed to return. Several parachutes had been seen, but there was no definite news.

After quickly refuelling and rearming, four of the pilots, including Johnnie Johnson, took off again to fly over and search the coast off the Pas de Calais in case Douglas or Buck were down in the sea. Air Sea Rescue was also alerted and enquiries were made at all possible aerodromes back in Southern England where they might have landed.

It was two days later that Woody got a call from someone at the Air Ministry to say that a message in plain language had been intercepted from the Germans to say that Wing Commander Bader was in St Omer hospital. He was not badly hurt, but his right artificial leg had been damaged. The

Photographed a few weeks after Bader was shot down, Johnnie Johnson's fighter has painted on its engine cover "Bader's Bus Co. - Still Running" in tribute to his missing commander.

message went on to say that safe conduct would be guaranteed to an unarmed aircraft that could fly a spare leg to a designated aerodrome.

Woody immediately telephoned Douglas's wife Thelma to give her the good news. He also started to make plans to fly over to France himself and to personally deliver Douglas's spare leg. This plan was vetoed by Leigh-Mallory, who pointed out that the offer of safe conduct could actually be a subtle propaganda move.

Douglas got his spare leg, but it was dropped during a normal bombing raid on the next Circus operation. The leg was flown in one of the Blenheims that was escorted by the Spitfires of the Tangmere Wing. A special box was constructed to hold the leg and as they flew over St Omer, this was dropped by parachute before the aircraft flew on to their target about 20 miles further inland.

In fact the spare leg arrived after the German technician had repaired the damaged one and after Douglas had managed to escape from the hospital by shinning down a rope made from knotted sheets. What he didn't know was that plans had already been put in place to spirit him away from the hospital in a fake ambulance and then send a Lysander aircraft over to France to collect him.

His pre-emptive solo attempt spoilt all this and although he manage to make contact with the local resistance, his minders were betrayed and he was back in captivity again.

It is not hard to understand the dismay and near panic in the Air Ministry when news came of Douglas's 'failure to return'. He was, after all, one of the RAF's most famous pilots and a priceless PR asset. He had reached a level of fame where people would actually stop him in the street and ask him for his autograph.

Sholto Douglas's immediate reaction when he heard the news was: "Oh God, no!" He considered that the loss of Douglas would be a tremendous blow to the morale of his pilots. It also presented a serious problem of who would now lead the Tangmere Wing.

Douglas had never been one for delegation and had always insisted on leading every mission himself. In many respects this had worked well. Laddie Lucas pointed out that day after day Douglas "contrived to keep the wing together and to get it to the right place at the right time without any fuss. The attributes that he brought to his command were readily discernable."

The lack of delegation that had prevented anyone else from gaining experience had not been treated as any particular problem because few people ever considered that anything could happen to Douglas the Invincible. It was virtually unthinkable that this pattern of operation should ever come to an end, but it inevitably did.

Douglas had been an exacting taskmaster and there were some who were secretly glad to see the back of him but for nearly everyone he was a dreadful loss. Most people remembered him for his outstanding and inspiring leadership qualities. Johnnie Johnson described him as "a wing leader par excellence, the unrivalled tactician, the man who knew it all - and was able to teach it all. When he was gone … the void was always there. It was never filled in my time."

Between 24th March and 9th August, the day he was shot down, Douglas had flown 62 consecutive sweeps or offensive operations over enemy territory. In most cases he was accompanied by the other three members of his usual two-pair formation; Hugh (Cocky) Dundas, Johnnie Johnson and Alan Smith.

Douglas may have been criticized for his lack of delegation, but through his own qualities of leadership he was obviously able to bring out such qualities in others with whom he came into contact. As Laddie Lucas put it, Douglas had a leadership quality that enabled him consciously or unconsciously to stamp his model on others.

Both Cocky Dundas and Johnnie Johnson went on to become two of the RAF's best-known and most successful wing leaders. Sergeant Alan Smith, Douglas's dependable wingman, was later commissioned and served with distinction as a flight commander in North Africa and after more than 20 confirmed 'kills' became an instructor in both the UK and the US.

After the war Alan Smith and Cocky Dundas both went on to become 'captains of industry' and both received knighthoods. Johnnie Johnson remained in the RAF to retire as a highly decorated Air Vice-Marshall in 1966.

Stan Turner, the stroppy Canadian Pilot Officer whom Douglas first encountered when he took over 242 Squadron, went on to become CO of 145 Squadron as part of Douglas's Tangmere Wing. Later he was instrumental in transforming the flying in Malta and by December 1943 he was also a wing commander during the Allies' northerly advance through Italy. He transferred the RCAF in 1944 and he too stayed in the service after the ending of hostilities.

Tim Vigors, the young pilot who had helped Douglas deliver the original Spitfires to 222 Squadron fought with distinction in the Far East, rising to the rank of wing commander, before leaving the RAF at the end of the war. From the 1960s he was a leading figure in the racing world and the bloodstock industry.

Sir Alan Smith who died in March 2013 at the age of 96 was one of the last survivors who had served with Douglas.. The year before he died he had this to say: "Douglas was very logical and very sensible. He was a marvellous leader, a brilliant pilot, a dead shot and everything you relish. He didn't just save my life, he saved a hell of a lot of lives."

The PoW

From the moment of his capture Douglas found himself having to make the difficult adjustment to life as a prisoner. For someone who had been used to making his own decisions and telling other people what to do, this was not an easy transition.

Captivity affected people in different ways. There were some who were fatalistic in their acceptance of captivity and tried to make the best of it, while others found it hard to accept captivity and did their best to escape and if escape proved impossible they did their best to annoy their captors. Douglas belonged to the second group.

He had made his first attempt to escape while he was still a patient in the hospital in St Omer, shinning down a homemade rope of knotted sheets before making contact with a French couple who agreed to help him. Unfortunately he was betrayed and recaptured.

After his recapture the Germans took no chances when Douglas was taken by train to Brussels and then onward to the Luftwaffe interrogation centre near Frankfurt-am-Main that was known as Dulag Luft. As he later put it: "They wouldn't give me my legs. Two goons carried me while another carried my legs and an officer marched along in front."

At Dulag Luft he immediately proved to be troublesome to his captors by refusing to answer any questions. When he was put into the adjacent transit camp he began to exert himself, telling his fellow captors that escape should be their passion and their one and only obsession until they reached home. The last straw for the Germans was his utter refusal to salute any German officer who was of lower rank than himself. They couldn't wait to be rid of him and he was promptly transferred to a POW camp for officers at Lübeck, Oflag XC.

Since Douglas was so famous the Germans tried to make the most of the potential propaganda value of having him, but he refused to be anything other than bloody-minded.

In October 1941 the RAF prisoners were transferred to Oflag VIB at Warburg. This was also a 'hut and wire camp', but the roofs of the huts leaked and it was seriously overcrowded. There never seemed to be enough light or fuel, the whole place became a sea of mud when it rained and in spite of a delivery of Red Cross parcels, food was always in short supply.

Douglas had always had enormous reserves of pent up energy. Up until 1931 this energy had been dissipated by sport, then he had his accident. Ten years later aerial combat and aerobatics had been providing the substitute, but now he had been deprived of that as well. As a POW he devised two alternative outlets; one was scheming to escape and the other was annoying the Germans.

Escaping was obviously a problem. His walk made him instantly recognisable and since he couldn't run or climb it would be impossible to go over or through the wire. It seemed that the only option of escape was by means of a tunnel.

The trouble with tunnels was that they took a long time to complete and were often discovered. They were also enterprises in which it was difficult for Douglas to actively participate. In spite of this, he was involved in several escape attempts as well as being involved in a number of diversions while other escape attempts were being made.

Douglas also became a past master of what was known as 'goon baiting', or doing one's best to make the Germans look foolish. On one snowy morning he refused to get out of bed to attend roll call. When a German officer came to fetch him he still refused, saying that his feet would get cold in the snow. It was only when the furious officer pulled out his pistol and threatened to shoot him that Douglas finally agreed to get up.

Other prisoners tended to have mixed opinions about Douglas's behaviour. While some thought that his antics were good for morale, others were simply irritated. As a fellow RAF prisoner later diplomatically put it, "he did not receive an unalloyed welcome from all". There was a feeling among a number of prisoners that life was bad enough anyway, so why make it worse by simply antagonising the captors.

As something of a star prisoner, Douglas was never seriously punished, although there were a couple of times when he pushed the guards to the point where they were about to open fire on the assembled prisoners and it was only as a result of some delicate negotiation that the situation was defused.

It was quite clear to everyone that Douglas was completely self-centred and simply "didn't care a damn for anybody".

Oflag VIB accommodated both army and RAF officers, but in May 1942 it was decided that the RAF prisoners were to be moved out and transferred under guard to a new camp run by the Luftwaffe, Stalag Luft III at Sagan. This was a huge camp and initially Douglas was housed in the NCO's compound where his goon baiting soon resulted in retaliation in the form of extended head-count parades and loss of privileges. This drew a mixed reaction from the other prisoners and on the whole they were pleased when Douglas was transferred to the officer's compound.

Here Douglas continued his antics. As one of his fellow hut-mates put it, the Germans had a great deal of respect for Douglas and they would put up with more from him than from anyone else, but when he went too far, the prisoners would all suffer from the collective retribution that would result. Incoming and outgoing mail might be held up, or the supply of Red Cross parcels might be interrupted simply because Douglas had refused to stand in front of the commandant or had insulted a German officer.

As a result of the way that they had suffered because of Douglas's behaviour, there were some RAF officers who came to detest him to the point that in later years they could not even bear to hear the mention of his name.

Douglas was still determined to escape, but his artificial legs were an obvious problem, so he devised an escape plan that he was convinced would work. First he had to get out of the camp and once outside he would simply steal an aeroplane and fly home. It all sounded very simple, but unfortunately the only way he could get out was through a tunnel and the escape committee would not agree to his taking part for fear of slowing down the others.

Douglas found it galling because for the first time in a long while he was not in charge of things. It was Wing Commander Harry (Wings) Day, Douglas's old mentor from 23 Squadron and the Hendon Air Pageant days who was the Senior British Officer and not Douglas. Although they were both wing commanders Harry Day was the more senior of the two.

It was also Harry's role as Senior British Officer to appoint and support the escape committee. This brought a further problem for Douglas. He was always very conscious of the hierarchy of rank and as a wing commander he was furious to be told what he could and could not do by an escape committee made up of officers who were more junior in rank to him.

After the war it was reported that Douglas actually lodged an official complaint for insubordination against one of the survivors of the Great Escape because he had not let him get his own way.

After a while the camp commandant at Stalag Luft III was at the end of his tether with Douglas's antics. The commandant was actually a very reasonable man and he sent for Wing Commander Day and asked for his advice. Day told the commandant that Douglas was an energetic man who was unable to dissipate his energy through sport in the usual way and his difficult attitude was his only alternative.

It was decided that Douglas should be transferred again, this time to Stalag VIIIB at Lamsdorf. This was a huge camp for British Army soldiers and where there was a significant number of British medical officers. Needless to say, when the day came to move, Douglas refused to budge.

On 10th July a detachment of 50 heavily armed guards arrived to escort him. He still refused to go and the situation began to look quite ugly. It was only after Wing Commander Day intervened to defuse the situation that Douglas finally agreed to leave.

At Lamsdorf he continued to be a nuisance to his captors. He made several unsuccessful escape attempts and managed to irritate as many prisoners as those who came to admire him. Following his final escape attempt he was thrown into solitary confinement. After staying there for ten days he was informed that he was to be transferred to Colditz Castle.

Through the interpreter Douglas announced that he was prepared to go to Colditz, but "I shall expect to travel first class and be accompanied by a batman and an officer of equal rank". After due consultation the interpreter returned and with a slight smile he relayed the commandant's response. "He says that he would be ready to meet all your points but he wants you to know that he is the only officer here of equal rank to you and he has other things to do."

Oflag IVC, otherwise known as Colditz Castle, was located about 30 miles southeast of Leipzig. When Douglas arrived there on 17th August 1942 he had been a POW for just over a year. Colditz was his sixth camp and it was here that he would spend the following two years and eight months until US troops liberated the camp on 16th April 1945.

Colditz was where the Germans sent persistent escapers and other troublemakers. It was a thousand-year-old fortress in the heart of Hitler's Reich, some four hundred miles from any frontier that was not under Nazi control. It was built on a cliff with a sheer drop of some 250 feet to the River Mulde below. The outer walls of the castle were seven feet thick and tunnelling was considered to be impossible.

At Colditz Douglas caught up with several old friends, including Geoffrey Stephenson and he discovered that many of them were just as determined to 'bait goons' as he was. This was well established by the time Douglas arrived, but he managed to take it to new heights. For instance

The castle at Colditz was established in 1046 though most of what stands today dates to the 16th century. After use as a royal residence by the Kings of Saxony the castle became a hospital in the 19th century and then a prison during World War II.

he refused to salute the second in command on the commandant's staff on the grounds that he was only a major and thus of inferior rank to him. He would then make things worse by pointedly blowing pipe smoke into the German officer's face.

Douglas's skills were so finely honed that there began to be concerns that his relentless goon baiting might eventually backfire and produce a bloody confrontation. One of his fellow prisoners commented that he was the sort of person that you would follow into the jaws of Hell if you were flying a Spitfire, but he was possibly not someone that you would look to for calm and sober judgement.

As usual Douglas had passionate admirers, but as had been the case in his previous camps, there were others who couldn't stand him. This led to him being variously described as 'a marvellous chap', 'a bit of a pain in the neck' and 'a real bastard'.

He could also be extremely self-centred. An example of this occurred in 1943 involving his batman, Alec Ross. Ross had been a bandsman in the Seaforth Highlanders and had been assigned to Douglas while he was in the cells at Stalag VIIIB. Since he had become fed up with the dreariness of Lamsdorf Ross had asked if he could accompany Douglas to Colditz and Douglas had supported the move.

Although Douglas had become dependent on Ross to give him piggyback rides up and down the castle stairs, he still treated him very much like a below-stairs servant, although in all fairness he was like this with everyone of lower rank than himself. As Ross said, "he was very, very regimental. He was the boss. Wherever he was he liked to be the head one. When he shouted, you ran to do whatever he wanted.".

Bandsmen traditionally double as medical orderlies and a few months after arriving in Colditz Ross was told that since he was a non-combatant he was to be repatriated as part of one of the periodic prisoner exchanges. Ross was thrilled and when he told Douglas "I'm going home", the immediate response was, "No you're bloody not. You came here to be my skivvy and that's what you'll stay." After Douglas managed to block the move, Ross had to spend nearly two more years in Colditz 'skivvying' for Douglas when he could easily have gone home.

The end of captivity came on 16th April 1945 when the US Army entered the castle. Douglas spotted a female American reporter by the name of Lee Carson and immediately managed to get himself an interview. As a result, he was the first prisoner to leave. The Americans initially flew him to an airfield at Versailles, just outside Paris, where he was shown into the officers' mess and greeted by the commanding general himself who told him that there was a long-distance phone call waiting for him in the next room.

The Americans had managed to track down Thelma and had phoned her at the family home in Ascot. It was the first time that she and Douglas had spoken to each other in three and a half years. Douglas being Douglas told Thelma that he wouldn't be coming home just yet since he was looking for a Spitfire because "I want to have a last fling before the war packs up".

Fortunately the C-in-C Fighter Command had earlier had the foresight to circulate a message to say that under no circumstances was Douglas Bader to be allowed back into combat.

Douglas had left Colditz so abruptly that he had forgotten to take his spare set of legs. When he later phoned Alec Ross he discovered that his former servant had left them behind in Colditz. Douglas swore, hung up and never spoke to Ross ever again.

Still anxious to continue the fight Douglas tried to get a posting to the Far East to fight the Japanese but this also was vetoed on the grounds that his stumps would sweat and chaff in the heat.

He was offered and accepted a posting to head the Day Fighter Wing of the Central Flying Establishment with a rank of Group Captain starting on 1st June 1945. This appointment was a disaster. In the three and a half years that Douglas had been away, things had moved on, but unfortunately he was still thinking in terms of Spitfires and Hurricanes, while he was now in the world of Hawker Tempests and Gloster Meteors.

Tactics had also changed. The officers that flew under Douglas were all veterans who were more familiar with contemporary aircraft and tactics than he was. The pilots found him brusque and opinionated and rarely willing to listen to what anyone had to say. Six weeks was long enough and Douglas was wisely posted to take command of the North Weald Sector on 20th July 1945.

For Battle of Britain Day on 15th September 1945, Douglas was chosen to lead the first peacetime ceremonial flypast over London. Of all the pilots who had taken part in the Battle of Britain some 375 had been killed in action and fewer than 50 had survived until the end of the war. A number of those survivors took part in the flypast.

This in fact turned out to be Douglas's swansong as for as the RAF was concerned. Barely six months after his North Weald appointment the announcement came that Group Captain Douglas Bader, DSO and Bar, DFC and Bar, was being released from the RAF. He returned to civilian life in February 1946.

The reasons for his fairly sudden change of direction were never explained, but in the nine-month period after his release from Colditz Douglas had the chance to review his position and his future. After nearly four years as a POW he couldn't wait to get back into action, but he very soon came to realise that the post-war RAF lifestyle was going to be far removed from the swashbuckling life that he had been used to four or five years earlier.

Time more or less stands still for a POW and after his release Douglas continued to think in terms of the Battle of Britain and the Rhubarbs and Circuses of the Tangmere Wing. He found it difficult to get to grips with the new aircraft, the new tactics and the new ways of thinking of the developing Cold War. He had been out of touch for too long and effectively he was one of yesterday's men.

His great friend and patron, Trafford Leigh-Mallory, was no longer there to support him, having been killed in a plane crash in November 1944. This effectively deprived Douglas of all the influence in high places that had previously enabled him to get away with so much of his unorthodox behaviour. In other words he knew that in future with nobody there to speak up for him, he would simply have to tow the line.

He was also aware that many of the future involvements of the RAF would be 'East of Suez', but it had been made clear to him that he was to be barred from service in tropical locations because his legs would not be able to stand the heat and humidity. This ruling would obviously limit his prospects of promotion.

His years as a POW may also have influenced his decision. He must have been aware that while his 'goon baiting' antics might have been a bit of fun and broken the monotony, they had also made him a lot of enemies and that many of those whom he had antagonised were still in the service.

Kenneth More, who so memorably portrayed Douglas in the film Reach for the Sky, told a story of how after the film had been released, invitations began to pour in for him to speak at various functions. On one occasion in the late 1950s he was asked to speak at a Battle of Britain lunch at the RAF station in Andover. In the middle of lunch the CO leaned across and asked him what he was going to talk about.

More said he thought he would tell a few stories about Douglas Bader. The CO went puce and told More that under no circumstances was he ever to "mention that bastard's name in this mess. See him at the end of the table?" ranted the CO, "He was in the bag with Bader, so was he, and he, and he. They kept losing their f***ing Red Cross parcels because he was always trying to escape and annoy the Germans. Bloody silly!"

Although Douglas was not normally sensitive to this sort of thing, he was obviously aware of the depth of feeling among a number of his potential colleagues. If he were to remain in the service, their paths would undoubtedly cross, which could prove very difficult. It is reasonable to assume that this might have been yet another factor that influenced his decision to leave.

But perhaps it was the RAF that made the ultimate decision. Maybe the 'men at the ministry' felt that Douglas was too much of a loose cannon in the post war Royal Air Force. He had been just right during the cut and thrust of the Battle of Britain and the period immediately following, but that was very much a different world. Perhaps they were the ones who persuaded him to go; but once again, perhaps we will never know.

Post-War
Adjustment

Douglas was still only 36 when he left the Royal Air Force for a second time and apart from those few years when he worked for Shell in the 1930s, the RAF had ruled his life since he had first entered Cranwell 18 years earlier.

In common with countless men of his generation his most pressing problem when he left the service was that of earning a living. Friends had suggested to him that he should stand for election as a Member of Parliament, but there was mutual agreement that he would not be suitable for any position other than Prime Minister. Fortunately the heads of Shell Oil were happy to have him back in their aviation department and he rejoined the company in July 1946 and was to stay with Shell for the next 23 years.

From the company's point of view, having such a war hero on their payroll was a great PR asset, but it was doubly useful because in those post-war days Douglas knew just about everyone in the aviation world and if he didn't know them personally, he would know someone who did.

At Shell he was more or less his own boss. His primary responsibilities in the early days were dealing with refuelling arrangements on airfields and the design and provision of equipment. Essentially this was the means by which the company's customers could ensure that their aircraft were refuelled.

This involved flying all over Europe and North Africa and later to the Far East. The company gave him a little two-seater, single-engined Hunting Percival Proctor V. This had a cruising speed of 120 mph and a flying duration of about five hours. The navigational aids were very limited and there was a very basic four-channel VHF radio.

For the Far Eastern trip he took Thelma and they set off from Croydon on 4th October 1948, intending to return by 10th or 12th December in time for Christmas. The five-hour flying duration made short hops a necessity and by degrees they made it to Bahrain, Karachi, Delhi, Singapore, Borneo and Java. This was all new territory for Douglas, where not only did he have to cope with navigation, but also the meteorological problems associated with monsoons.

Obviously in a little single-engined aircraft there was no way that he could fly over the bad weather in the way a modern airliner would, so he simply had to fly under the towering banks of cumulus clouds.

After the war, Bader was keen to see combat aircraft preserved for future generations. Seen here is Hurricane Mk1 serial R4118 which flew with No.605 Squadron during the Battle of Britain and is the Battle of Britain Hurricane still in flying condition.

After spending ten days in Borneo, on 11th November Douglas and Thelma set course from Java for home. When they stopped in Oman, Douglas had the first of many encounters that he was to have with people with disabilities that were going to have such a profound effect on his future personal life and his future time with Shell.

In those days Oman was a British Protectorate and the Sultan had a small army of Baluchi tribesmen with British officers. Douglas discovered that three of the Baluchi had lost legs in local operations, chiefly as a result of treading on mines. He discovered that although they had been working on behalf of the British government, the War Office had taken no responsibility for them because it was the Sultan who employed and paid them. Douglas resolved to do something about this when he got back home.

Douglas and Thelma arrived home from their trip in the middle of the afternoon of 11th December. They had travelled some 9,000 miles, completed 23 separate landings, made 18 overnight stops and flown 79 flying hours in a 120 mph single-engined aeroplane with minimal navigational aids.

One of his first acts following his return was to try to do something for the limbless Baluchi warriors in Oman. After getting no joy from the War Office or from any other government department, he approached his bosses in Shell. The company offered to pay for artificial limbs, but said that they would have to appear to come from Douglas as a present from him because Shell couldn't be seen to be directly involved.

Using his contacts, Douglas arranged for casts to be taken of the men's legs, for the hospital at Roehampton to make the limbs and for BOAC to fly them out. When Douglas next visited he reported how these 'marvellous chaps were absolutely thrilled and went round the room high-kicking like storm troopers'. This was a foretaste of what was to come and for many years people all over the world began to walk around on artificial legs after Douglas had identified a need. Nobody ever knew that as a result of Douglas's influence, the legs had all been funded by Shell.

In 1954 a new chapter of Douglas's life began when Paul Brickhill's book, Reach for the Sky was published. Brickhill was an Australian journalist who had flown with the RAAF and had been a prisoner in Stalag Luft III. His first book, The Great Escape told of the mass breakout from the camp that had ended in tragedy after Hitler personally ordered 50 of the recaptured escapees to be shot. Brickhill followed this book with another big hit, The Dam Busters, that told the story of Operation Chastise when aircraft from 617 Squadron used a specially designed bouncing bomb to destroy some vital dams in the Ruhr.

Brickhill's third book, Reach for the Sky also became an instant best seller. It came out early in the year, selling 100,000 copies on publication and by early June it had sold another 72,000. Rather than take a royalty, for his contribution towards the book Douglas had taken a one-off payment of £10,000 for all rights, which in today's money would be equivalent to something over £190,000. Douglas and Thelma put the money towards the purchase of a small mews house off Queen's Gate in South Kensington where they were to spend the remaining 15 of their 37 years together.

Considering that this one-off payment included all film rights and taking into account the fact that after nearly 60 years the book is still in print, £10,000 might not have been such a good deal after all, but without it Douglas and Thelma would never have been able to purchase the house in Queen's Gate.

The film version of course was inevitable and the actor chosen to play Douglas was Kenneth More. It is said that Kenneth More was actually the second choice for the lead after the first choice, Richard Burton, dropped out. Several of More's friends, including Alexander Korda and Lawrence Olivia tried to warn him off, saying that the part was not right for him but Kenneth More was confident that it was and the final result proved that his judgement was sound. He was apparently paid £25,000 for the role.

Douglas and Kenneth only met twice before shooting started. The first time was when they had lunch together and talked for a couple of hours and the second was when they went up to Gleneagles and played a round of golf on the same day. Kenneth More was a very good golfer and was quite astonished when Douglas decisively beat him. To an actor of Kenneth More's calibre these meetings were all that he needed to fix the image of Douglas in his mind. He told Douglas that if there were any more meetings he would be in danger of caricaturing Douglas rather than portraying him.

In later years the two became good friends and often played golf together. Douglas was always highly amused that when they walked down the fairway Kenneth always seemed to unconsciously adopt Douglas's way of walking.

Once filming started things did not always go smoothly. Douglas was keen to see all the real-life characters individually represented in the film and for everything to be exactly as it happened. In the end he had to accept that of necessity some things had to be changed otherwise the film would end up with a confusing number of characters.

Douglas was particularly upset when he read the script to see that in the scene of the crash, Geoffrey Stephenson rather than Jack Cruttenden was portrayed as being the one who lifted him out of the wreckage and saved is life by keeping a firm pressure on his femoral artery as they travelled to hospital in the ambulance.

Finally filming was finished, but then came another big problem, this time not through Douglas's making. A message in the opening credits carries the clue. "It has been necessary to reshape some of the characters involved in this story. The producers apologise to those who may have been affected by any changes or omissions."

Douglas's old friend Geoffrey Stephenson had stayed in the RAF after the war and in November 1954 was an Air Commodore with the Central Fighter Establishment at RAF West Raynham in Norfolk. On 8th November, while he was heading a 6-man team to Elgin Air Force Base in Florida, he was flying an F-100 Super Sabre, when his aircraft dived into a pine forest and he was killed. When Geoffrey's family saw a preview of the film early in 1956, they took great exception to the way that he had been portrayed by the actor Lyndon Brook. Obviously at this late stage the character could not be removed from the film, but as a compromise it was agreed to change his name.

As a result, Geoffrey Stephenson became a fictional character by the name of Johnnie Sanderson. This required a certain amount of dubbing to the sound track and a careful look at Kenneth More's lip movements whenever he says Johnnie, will show quite clearly that what he is actually saying is Geoffrey.

The prestigious World Première of the film took place on 5th July 1956 at London's Odeon Theatre Leicester Square. This was a charity event in the presence of Prince Philip, but Douglas refused to go. The film was regarded as a triumph, but years passed before he eventually came to see it.

Douglas was pretty well known before Reach for the Sky, but after its release he was really famous and became a household name. For some people this would have gone to their heads, but Douglas continued to behave exactly as he had always done. At times he could still be unreasonable and unthinkingly difficult, while at other times he was charm personified.

Laddie Lucas, his brother-in-law, describes how with families, friends and colleagues, one moment he could be preposterously dominant and assertive, while the next minute he would be winning, generous, engaging and loyal.

Then, after many years where Douglas had seemed to have completely shut the film out of his mind, one evening the film was shown on television. To his family's utter astonishment he actually sat through it to the end. When the final credits had finished rolling, someone timorously asked him what he had thought of it. He apparently took two matches to light his pipe before replying: "Rather good old boy". He then changed the subject.

The Lasting Legacy

In the years that he worked for Shell Douglas travelled all over the world. Since he was more less his own boss, this left him plenty of time for his charity work and his work for disabled people. As ever, he was always very demanding, but from Shell's point of view his plusses exceeded his minuses. Douglas was a great asset to the company in many ways. In addition to being a war hero that everybody knew about, from Shell's point of view this high profile larger than life character had an encyclopaedic number of contacts and was able to gain access to countless numbers of people and open doors that would otherwise have remained firmly shut.

His downside was that he was often outspoken and from time to time was a considerable embarrassment to his company. He had always believed in speaking his mind and he was inclined to say things and do things without giving any thought to the possible implications or consequences of what he was doing or saying.

A good example was when in 1952 he was approached by an Irish publisher and asked if he would write the foreword to Stuka Pilot, the English

Hans Rudel, the Luftwaffe pilot whose memoirs landed Bader in trouble in 1952.

language version of the memoirs of a former Luftwaffe pilot called Hans Ulrich Rudel. Rudel had lost a leg during the war and had refused to be grounded, so obviously his story was dear to Douglas's heart. Without reading the manuscript Douglas gladly agreed to comply.

Rudel was actually the most highly decorated German serviceman of the war and the only person to be awarded Germany's highest military decoration, the Knight's Cross of the Iron Cross with Golden Oak Leaves, Swords and Diamonds. He had flown 2,530 combat missions and claimed a total of 2,000 targets destroyed, including 519 tanks and a Soviet battleship.

Unfortunately Rudel had also been a dedicated Nazi and his sympathies certainly had changed very little following the ending of the war. This fact was quite clear from the text of the book, but of course Douglas didn't know this because he hadn't read the manuscript. As if this wasn't bad enough the book's Irish publishing house had connections with the pre-war British Union of Fascists.

It must be remembered that these events were taking place just seven years after the ending of the war and feelings were still running very high. As soon as the book was published this was all picked up by the British press, but Douglas was unrepentant, maintaining that he only wrote what he did because he admired a fellow flyer. He apparently failed to appreciate that this was an action that could easily have linked him and potentially his employer to extremist far-right politics.

His 'gaffs', as they would now be called, continued over the years and there must have been occasions when he had Shell's PR department running around in circles. It was not surprising that when Douglas come to apply for the vacancy of senior personnel manager, his application was turned down flat.

Another crisis for the company occurred on one of Douglas's last trips to southern Africa in late 1965. It was just after the Rhodesian Prime Minister and former RAF officer, Ian Smith, had declared Rhodesia's Universal Declaration of Independence (UDI) from the United Kingdom.

The Rhodesian Government maintained that since it had governed itself since 1923 it should be granted independence in the same way as other former African colonies. The problem was that the Rhodesian government was a white minority government and the British government's position was "no independence before majority rule".

Douglas attended a function and gave an address where he was very vocal in his support of Ian Smith. UDI had just been introduced following the imposition of economic sanctions by the British government and Douglas's pointed assault on the British government's policy resulted in UK headlines such as: "Shell Chief Blasts Sanctions – Bader's Outspoken Attack".

The managing director of Shell was not pleased and on his return to the UK Douglas was called in for an interview where it was pointed out to him that firstly he was not a 'Shell chief' and secondly there was a need for him to take account of corporate interests whenever he made a speech in public.

Douglas finally retired from Shell in 1969, a few months short of his 60th birthday. By then he had clocked up a total of 5,360 flying hours in his log book. Of those, 3,900 had been completed in the 23 years that he had worked for Shell after the war. It was said the during that period there wasn't another pilot anywhere in the world who had greater all-round experience of flying and navigating light aircraft.

His last 850 flying hours with Shell had been completed in a Beech 95 Travelair. Although it was a single-engined aircraft, with its modern aids it was in a different league to the Proctor V that he and Thelma had used for their epic journey to the Far East in 1948. On his retirement Shell presented him with the Travelair as a parting gift. It was an appropriate time for Douglas to retire. The pace of his hectic lifestyle was beginning to tell and two years earlier Thelma had begun to develop emphysema. She had always been a heavy smoker and although by now she had stopped smoking, it was too late to help her and she was showing signs of getting worse. Aware that her survival was unlikely, the two spent as much time with each other as possible. and after a long battle she died on 24th January 1971. They had been married for 37 years.Thelma had always been a popular hostess at the many gatherings of pilots that had been held at their home. The pilots held a true affection for her and the RAF church of St Clement Danes was packed for her thanksgiving service on 6th March. The Address to the capacity congregation was delivered by Marshal of the Royal Air Force Sir Dermot Boyle and that night London's Evening News carried the headline: "The Few Salute Thelma Bader". Thelma had always been a great support to Douglas and he found that golf helped him to deal with his loss.

It was golf that brought him to his second wife. He had met Joan Murray some years before when they were partnered in a golfing competition organised in support of the British Limbless Ex-Serviceman's Association. She had taken the place of Douglas's original partner who had to drop out.Joan and Douglas were married quietly on 3rd January 1963 in a church near Coventry. The vicar, the Reverend Tom Knight, was yet another of Douglas's friends. In a former life Tom Knight had been a Group Captain in charge of a bomber station. Like Douglas, Joan had a great interest in helping people with disabilities. In addition to her involvement with the British Limbless Ex-Serviceman's Association, she was also one of the original volunteer supporters of Riding for the Disabled, of which Douglas was an honorary life president.

Following their marriage Douglas and Joan received countless invitations to speak and to attend events. They continued to fulfil engagements all over the world although long journeys were now made by commercial airliners and not by private aircraft. In most cases the main purpose of their journey was to assist in the cause of the disabled and they continued to campaign vigorously for people with disabilities. Douglas was a perfect example of how a disability could be overcome and both knew that by meeting people with disabilities he could plainly demonstrate what was possible.

The Battle of Britain Monument which stands on the Victoria Embankment in central London. It was erected in 2005 to commemorate the heroism of the pilots, ground crew and others who saved Britain in the Battle of Britain.

In June 1976 Douglas received a knighthood for his services to disabled people. This could have been a great embarrassment, because protocol dictated that one had to kneel while being dubbed with the sword. Douglas knew that this would be a recipe for disaster because he would certainly fall flat on his face. As a result he was given special dispensation from the Queen to receive his knighthood standing up.

Other awards were to follow. Despite his charity work Douglas still found time to maintain his interest in aviation and in 1977 he was made a Fellow of the Royal Aeronautical Society.

As the decade moved on, Douglas's health began to decline and in 1979 he made the decision to finally give up flying. His workload was exhausting for a legless man and he had a worsening heart condition. Four months after his 69th birthday, on 4th June 1979, he made his final flight in his little Beech 95 Travelair. His log book recorded a total flying time of 5,744 hours and 25 minutes. Coincidentally his friend and former foe Adolf Galland decided to follow Douglas into aviation retirement shortly afterwards for the same reasons.

On 5 September 1982, about six months after his 72nd birthday, Douglas was guest speaker at a dinner honouring Marshal of the Royal Air Force Sir Arthur "Bomber" Harris in London's Guildhall. As he was being driven home he suffered a massive heart attack as they passed through Chiswick. Douglas never recovered.

On Wednesday 27th October his memorial service packed St Clement Danes. Many dignitaries and personalities attended, including the Prime Minister, Margaret Thatcher. Adolf Galland was on a business trip in California, but was determined to be in London for the service so that he could pay his final respects.

Douglas's legacy was felt to be too precious to simply be allowed to fade away so following his death a number of family and friends formed the Douglas Bader Foundation with a mission to continue his work in conjunction with and on behalf of individuals with a disability. The Foundation exists to advance and promote the physical, mental and spiritual welfare of persons who are without one or more limbs, or who are otherwise physically disabled. After thirty years the Foundation continues to thrive, with an annual golf tournament being one of the highlights.

72 years is not a particularly long life, but Douglas would probably have been the first to point out that his life was a damn sight longer that that of many of his contemporaries of the 1940s. His achievements were manifold and he touched the lives and had a major influence on thousands of people. While it is true that from time to time his sometimes forthright manner upset people, this was far outweighed by his many positive qualities.

As is the case with many famous people, he is commemorated by a Blue Plaque on the wall of the house that he shared with Thelma in Petersham Mews in Kensington, but this is only the start of it. Schools, roads and even pubs were also named after him. These include Bader Ways near the former airfield at Woodley where he had his accident, with another near the old RAF station at Hornchurch and yet another close to RAF Kirton in Lindsey. There is also a Bader Close is near the former RAF Kenley. There are schools in Auckland, New Zealand and Edmonton, Alberta both named after him and another on the former Coltishall RAF base. The 'Douglas Bader' pub is on the site of the former RAF Martlesham Heath and the 'Bader Arms' is in the village of Tangmere close to the former airfield.

Ten months before he died he was castaway on radio's Desert Island Discs. Included in his choice of eight 'gramophone records' were Richard Tauber singing Vienna City of my Dreams in German and Vera Lynn

Bader stands on the wing of his Hurricane fighter when he was commander of No.242 Squadron.

singing Lilli Marlene in English. His final record, obviously a reflection of his world travels was I'd Like To Teach the World To Sing by The New Seekers. For his luxury item he chose his favourite sand iron and some golf balls.

George Unwin and Gordon Sinclair were both members of 19 Squadron where Douglas was posted after he rejoined the RAF in February 1940. George Unwin, a sergeant-pilot at the time described him as "outstanding" and "an inspiration", while the ever-tactful Gordon Sinclair, a friend and squash partner of Douglas, commented in beautiful understatement that he "was not everyone's cup of tea."

Douglas was certainly different things to different people, but without a doubt he was one of the RAF's greatest heroes. He lived his life to the full and with some justification it could be said that his entire life was heroic.

Bibliography

Air Battle for Dunkirk 26 My – 3 June by Norman Franks – Grub Street

Bader's War by S P Mackenzie – Spellmount

Battle of Britain A Day by Day Chronicle by Patrick Bishop - Quercus

Battle of Britain by Len Deighton – Jonathan Cape

Fighter Boys by Patrick Bishop – Harper Collins

Flying Colours by Laddie Lucas – Hutchinson

Life's Too Short To Cry by Tim Vigors – Grub Street

Soldier, Sailor & Airman Too by AB 'Woody' Woodhall – Grub Street

Spitfire Squadron by Dilip Sarkar – Air Research Publications

The Bader Wing by John Frayn Turner – Pen and Sword

The Battle of Britain 50 Years On by Michael Bowyer – Patrick Stephens

The Battle of Britain by James Alexander – Transatlantic Press

The Battle of Britain the making of a film by Leonard Mosley – Weidenfeld & Nicolson

The Few by Philip Kaplan & Richard Collier – Blandford Press

The Fighter Pilots by Edward Sims – Cassell

The Narrow Margin by Derek Wood with Derek Dempster – Hutchinson

Wing Leader by Johnnie Johnson – Chatto and Windus

Winged Victory by Johnnie Johnson and Laddie Lucas – Random House